Immigration and American Religion

Religion in American Life

JON BUTLER & HARRY S. STOUT
GENERAL EDITORS

Immigration and American Religion

Jenna Weissman Joselit

UNIVERSITY PRESS

OXFORD
UNIVERSITY PRESS

Oxford   New York
Athens Auckland Bangkok Bogotá Buenos Aires Calcutta
Cape Town Chennai Dar es Salaam Delhi Florence Hong Kong Istanbul
Karachi Kuala Lumpur Madrid Melbourne Mexico City Mumbai
Nairobi Paris São Paulo Singapore Taipei Tokyo Toronto Warsaw
and associated companies in
Berlin Ibadan

Copyright © 2001 by Jenna Weissman Joselit

Published by Oxford University Press, Inc.
198 Madison Avenue, New York, New York 10016
www.oup.com

Oxford is a registered trademark of Oxford University Press

Library of Congress Cataloging-in-Publication Data

Joselit, Jenna Weissman.
  Immigration and American religion/Jenna Weissman Joselit.
    p. com. — (Religion in American life)
  Includes bibliographical references and index.
  ISBN 0-19-511083-8
  1.Immigrants—Religious life—United States—Juvenile literature. 2.United States—
  Emigration and immigration—Religious aspects—Juvenile literature.
  [1. Immigrants—Religious life. 2. United States—Emigration and immigration—
  Religious aspects.] I. Title. II. Series.

BL2525.J678   2001
200'.86'910973—dc21   00-060645

ISBN 0-19-511083-8

9 8 7 6 5 4 3 2 1

Printed in the United States of America
on acid-free paper

Design and layout: Loraine Machlin
Picture research: Lisa Kirchner, Jennifer Smith

On the cover: Irish immigrants disembark in New York harbor; painting by Samuel Waugh (1855).
Frontispiece: All Saints' Day festival in the North End of Boston, Massachusetts (1929).

Contents

Editors' Introduction

JON BUTLER & HARRY S. STOUT, GENERAL EDITORS

n America, the immigrant experience often has been the religious experience. From the 16th to the 21st centuries, immigrants have arrived in America fleeing religious persecution. Others found strength in religion as they faced a strange, enticing environment. Religion supported powerful institutions, secular and spiritual alike, that fostered immigrant ethnic identity. Everywhere religion shaped the immigrant social experience, from war and social reform to politics, family, and work.

Immigrants created new churches, synagogues, and mosques. They adapted rituals and traditions to fit the style of a new land. They discovered new ways of thinking about religion, new ways of arguing about religion, and new ways of proclaiming religion. And their battles against religious prejudice gave the First Amendment's guarantees of religious freedom new life and renewed meaning.

This book is part of a unique 17-volume series that explores the evolution, character, and dynamics of religion in American life from 1500 to the end of the 20th century. As late as the 1960s, historians paid relatively little attention to religion beyond studies of New England's Puritans. But since then, American religious history and its contemporary expression have been the subject of intense inquiry. These new studies have thoroughly transformed our knowledge of almost every American religious group and have fully revised our understanding of religion's role in U.S. history.

This 1917 poster for U.S. government bonds appealed to recent immigrants, who had now tasted freedom in America, to support the war effort.

It is impossible to capture the flavor and character of the American experience without understanding the connections between secular activities and religion. Spirituality stood at the center of Native American societies before European colonization and has continued to do so long after. Religion—and the freedom to express it—motivated millions of immigrants to come to the United States from remarkably different cultures, and the exposure to new ideas and ways of living shaped their experience. It also fueled tension among different ethnic and racial groups in the United States and, regretfully, accounted for difficult episodes of bigotry in American society. Religion urged Americans to expand the nation— first within the continental United States, then through overseas conquests and missionary work—and has had a profound influence on American politics, from the era of the Puritans to the present. Finally, religion contributes to the extraordinary diversity that has, for four centuries, made the United States one of the world's most dynamic societies.

The Religion in American Life series explores the historical traditions that have made religious freedom and spiritual exploration central features of American society. It emphasizes the experience of religion in America—what men and women have understood by religion, how it has affected politics and society, and how Americans have used it to shape their daily lives.

Religion in American Life

JON BUTLER & HARRY S. STOUT
GENERAL EDITORS

Preface

"Do not go to America," warned Rabbi Moses Weinberger in 1887, urging potential Jewish immigrants to stay home, in eastern Europe. In America, he said, nothing is as it ought to be. People violate the Sabbath, flout Judaism's dietary laws, and hardly ever go to synagogue. America is a godless place. Catholic leaders felt much the same way. "The atmosphere of America," one declared, "is laden with a deadly miasma [poisonous air] which has stifled the growth of the Church and wrought spiritual ruin." Even the Puritans, the founding mothers and fathers of our nation, had had their doubts. But they did not give in to them, nor did those who followed in their footsteps.

Since the early 17th century, millions of people from all over the world, from Lithuania to Laos, have turned a deaf ear to the naysayers and prophets of doom within their own communities. Seeking a better life for themselves and their families in America, they have braved an unfamiliar language, frighteningly new economic conditions, and sometimes considerable hostility and prejudice. Their cloth bundles and flimsy suitcases packed with tangible reminders of the world they were leaving behind, many immigrants made sure to bring their religion along with them. Some, of course, were so eager to put the Old World completely behind them that they threw off all its traces. Abandoning religion, they embraced a secular way of life. Most of them, however, held on to their faith, attempting—often at great financial and emotional cost—to

Dressed in their Sunday best and carrying all their worldly possessions with them, members of a young Italian family look forward to life in America as they ride the ferry from Ellis Island to Manhattan in 1904.

11

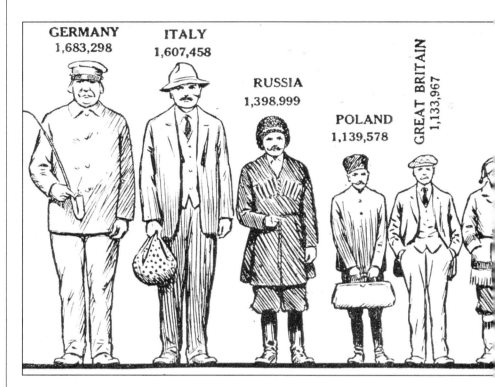

GERMANY
1,683,298

ITALY
1,607,458

RUSSIA
1,398,999

POLAND
1,139,578

GREAT BRITAIN
1,133,967

reestablish their cherished meetinghouses and mosques, synagogues, convents, and cathedrals in the New World. Some immigrants even became more religious, more attentive to ritual, than they had been at home. Here, in America, they discovered that religion was not only about God; it had to do with community and fellowship too.

Immigration not only changed people's lives, it also changed the meaning of religion. At first, American believers identified exclusively with Protestantism or one of its many variants. Over time, however, their ranks grew to include Catholics and Jews, Muslims and Buddhists, Hindus, Jains, and Sikhs, along with devotees of Santeria (a Cuban form of Catholicism) and Vodou (or voodoo, an African-derived, Haiti-based religion centering on ancestor worship and witchcraft). Expanding the number of believers, immigration increased the pool of priests, rabbis, imams (Muslim leaders), and babaloos (high priests of Santeria) who ministered to their souls. It also greatly enlarged the number of places where believers

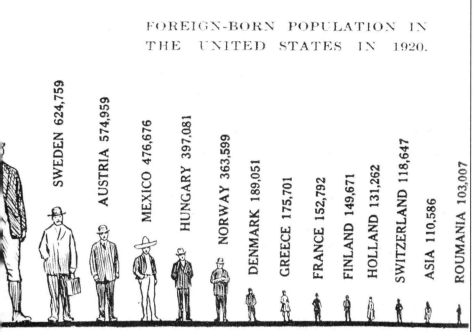

FOREIGN-BORN POPULATION IN THE UNITED STATES IN 1920.

SWEDEN 624,759
AUSTRIA 574,959
MEXICO 476,676
HUNGARY 397,081
NORWAY 363,599
DENMARK 189,051
GREECE 175,701
FRANCE 152,792
FINLAND 149,671
HOLLAND 131,262
SWITZERLAND 118,647
ASIA 110,586
ROUMANIA 103,007

The 1920 U.S. census showed a population of nearly 106 million people. As this chart illustrates, approximately 13 percent of that number were born in places other than the United States, mostly in European countries.

might practice their faith. The American religious landscape, first entirely empty of and then dominated by Protestant houses of worship, eventually came to make room for synagogues, cathedrals, and, by the late 20th century, mosques and Buddhist temples as well. Little by little, shrines, living rooms, and even the street, now the site of religious festivals and processions, also became a part of America's geography of faith.

Immigration affected religious time as well as space, augmenting the number of days during the week and occasions during the year when believers observed the Sabbath and other sacred moments. Where America's Protestants and Catholics, for instance, observe the Sabbath on Sunday, Muslims mark theirs on Friday and Jews on Saturday. What's more, the number of times during the year when special religious festivals are celebrated has also grown considerably, thanks to immigration. Along with Thanksgiving and Christmas, as well as Easter—a festival once shunned by Protestants but venerated by Catholics—the Islamic holy month of Ramadan, the Chinese New Year, and Rosh Hashanah (the Jewish New Year) have become fixtures of the American calendar.

To be sure, not every American welcomed these changes or, for that matter, the people who brought them. All too often, hostility rather than acceptance characterized the relationship between America and its immigrants. Some of the nation's citizens, their judgment clouded by prejudice, taunted the newcomers, burned their convents, expelled those who held beliefs different from their own, and enacted legislation that barred the Chinese and Japanese from entering the country and placed a severe quota or curb on the number of would-be immigrants from eastern Europe. It was only recently, in 1965, that this long-standing national tradition of restricting immigration was formally overturned.

Through it all, immigration has been, and continues to be, a central and defining feature of the American experience. Without the steady influx of millions of different people to these shores, we would not only be a very small and dull nation, we would not be America. What makes us unique, so unlike other places around the world, is the stunning diversity of the people who call this country home: Protestants from Britain; Lutherans from Scandinavia; Catholics from Ireland, Italy, and the Caribbean; Jews from eastern Europe; Muslims from the Middle East; Buddhists and Confucians from the Far East; and Sikhs and Jains from the Indian subcontinent. Every wave of immigrants, each in its own way, profoundly affected how and where Americans prayed and to whom. More to the point, virtually every facet of modern American life, from the schoolroom to the courts, the supermarket and the street, is rooted in the relationship between immigration and religion. Alive and well, that relationship is not just the stuff of family fables or history books. The interplay between religion and immigration touches all of us—in the sounds and rhythms of our prayers, the customs we hold dear, the foods we cherish, and even the way we decorate our homes and clothe ourselves.

How all this came to pass is the subject of this book, which draws on the voices and experiences of real-life immigrants as they struggled to find a balance between the claims of Old World tradition and the pressures of the New. Attentive to the similarities as well as differences among the various groups that came to America, it highlights the things that bound them together and those that set them apart. The book consists of a series of case studies, each of which focuses on either a distinctive moment in or a unique dimension of the American immigrant experience. Paying careful attention to changes over time from the early 17th century through the close of the 20th, the volume opens with the story of the Pilgrims and the Puritans, the first Protestant immigrants in the New World. A look at the various Protestant sects who succeeded them in the 18th century—groups like the Quakers, the Mennonites, and the Amish—follows, as does an inquiry into the lives of the immigrants who brought Lutheranism, another form of Protestantism, to the American heartland during the 19th century.

A second study considers the history of Catholicism and the efforts of the American Catholic Church throughout the 19th and 20th centuries to become a national church able to accommodate the spiritual and linguistic needs of an increasingly polyglot population. A third analysis, focusing largely on the 20th century, looks at the history of Jewish immigrants. Neither Catholic nor Protestant, they stood outside the framework of America's Christian character, testing the nation's openness to those of a different tradition. So too did immigrants from China, Japan, Korea, India, and the Middle East, the subject of the final case study. These groups, like the Jews before them, prompted contemporary Americans to think long and hard about the challenges of living in a pluralistic society.

Some readers may be disappointed not to find themselves or their immigrant parents or grandparents mentioned in this account. But if they make their way attentively through the text, perhaps they will recognize themselves all the same in the stories of those who do inhabit its pages. For when all is said and done, the story of America and its religions is the story of every immigrant.

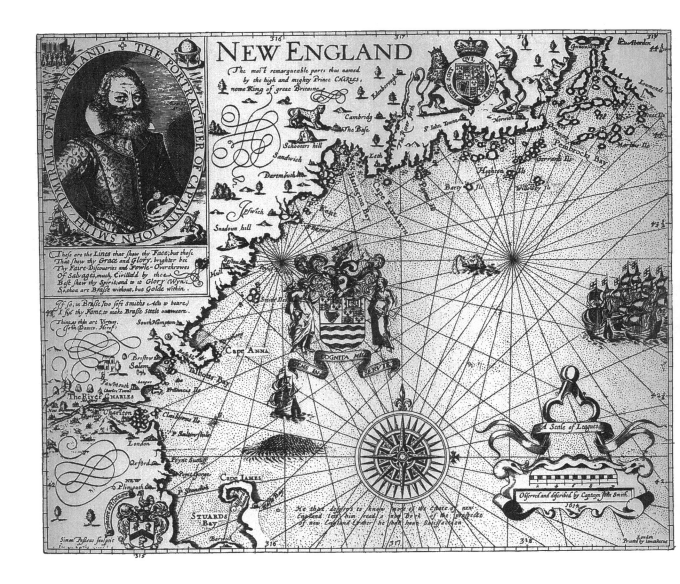

Chapter 1

The Free Air of the New World: The Protestant Immigrant Experience

Most of us go about our lives giving little thought to the Pilgrims or the Puritans, the 17th-century immigrants who, settling in what is now Massachusetts and Virginia, formed the very first generation of British colonists in North America. And when we do think of these two groups, usually (and fleetingly) at Thanksgiving, we tend to associate them, writes historian Edmund Morgan, with "kill-joys in tall-crowned hats, whose main occupation was to prevent each other from having any fun and whose sole virtue lay in their furniture." A closer look, however, at the people who proudly called themselves Pilgrims and Puritans—the Bradfords and the Winthrops, the Kembles and the Eddys—tells a different and far more complex story, one in which ordinary human beings, motivated by a profound sense of faith, set out to create a new kind of moral community amid the wilderness of the New World.

For the Pilgrims and the Puritans pulling up stakes and moving thousands of miles away to a place with none of the familiar comforts of home was an act born of courage, faith, and desperation. Before settling overseas at Plymouth Plantation in 1620, the Pilgrims, a Protestant sect whose rejection of the teachings and leadership of the Church of England led to their persecution, had tried establishing a new life for themselves in

The Old World could read about the New in books like John Smith's *A Description of New England*, published in London in 1616. This map from the book shows the locations of many of the British settlements in America, including Plymouth (Plimoth, lower left), named after Plymouth, England.

Holland. There, in Leiden, far from what they took to be England's characteristic ungodliness, they sought to practice their special brand of Protestantism. But Leiden turned out to be little better than London. According to the Pilgrim leader William Bradford, many of the community's children were "being drawn away by evil examples into extravagant courses, getting the reins off their necks and departing from their parents." Gravely concerned lest their sons and daughters reject the religion as well as the rule of their parents, the Pilgrims set their sights on and set sail for the "free aire of the new world."

The Chesapeake Bay area of Virginia, which had been colonized a few years earlier by Englishmen with decided Protestant leanings, was their destination. Perhaps it was Alexander Whitehead's 1613 sermon, "Good News from Virginia," in which the minister spoke enthusiastically of the colony's commitment to Protestantism, that inspired their choice of safe haven. Those who are "hot against the Surplis," he wrote, referring to the special white robe worn by Catholic priests, should come "hither" to Virginia, where it is not "spoken of." Or perhaps it was the prospect of living in a place where the law of the land not only ordered everyone to sanctify the Sabbath but severely punished those who did not. Whatever Virginia's attractions, the Pilgrims never made it there. Blown off course, their ship, the *Mayflower*, eventually dropped anchor way up north, in Provincetown Harbor, Massachusetts, in November 1620. A month later, the *Mayflower's* 102 passengers made their way to Plymouth Bay where, having agreed earlier in their travels to "covenant and combine ourselves into a civill body politick," they established a small community known as Plymouth Plantation.

A decade later, the Pilgrims were joined by the Puritans, members of a Protestant religious movement that had long sought to purify, rather than separate itself from, the Church of England. By the 1620s, though, as tensions between the Crown and Parliament multiplied, England's Puritan community no longer felt secure. Cherishing the vision of a new England where religious and political dissension might become a thing of the past, the Puritans sought "shelter and a hiding place for us and ours" in the New World. More to the point, they believed they had a special

In 1607, English emigrants cleared the swampy marshlands of Virginia and founded the colony of Jamestown, the first permanent British settlement in North America. One of the 144 settlers was the Reverend Robert Hunt, who led the newcomers in prayer upon their arrival.

destiny to play. Like the biblical Israelites of old, we Puritans have a mission, a "special commission," John Winthrop, the governor of the Massachusetts Bay Colony, told his fellow travelers aboard their ship, the *Arbella*. We have been singled out by God to serve as a "modell of Christian charity," to complete the process of reformation that had begun—and faltered—decades earlier. Here, in the wilderness that was the New World, the Puritans would start afresh by establishing a new kingdom of God, a kingdom administered and animated by Christian principles. At stake in this ambitious scheme was not just the well-being of one faraway colony but the future vitality of Protestantism. "For wee must Consider that wee shall be as a City upon a Hill, the eyes of all people are upon us," Winthrop told his followers. Should they fail, Winthrop warned, by "deal[ing] falsely with our God in this work . . . and so cause him to withdraw his present help from us, we shall be made a story and a by-word through the world."

Armed with high-minded principles as well as with a royal charter granting them the right to colonize the northeast coast of North America, some 900 men, women, and children landed in the tiny town of Salem in June 1630. They soon fanned out across the Charlestown peninsula, creating a network of settlements—Charlestown, Roxbury, Watertown, Newtown, Newbury, and Boston—that flew the banner of the Massachusetts Bay Colony. The first years were trying ones: Many immigrants, unaccustomed to the debilitating summer heat and the rigors of a New England winter, succumbed to starvation and disease. Others found it hard to make a go of it economically, while still others, disheartened by the harshness of colonial life, returned home to England.

Little by little, however, things improved. The Massachusetts Bay colonists learned to accommodate themselves to the weather and discovered what to plant and with whom to trade. A continuous stream of immigrants from the mother country helped sustain their efforts. Between 1630 and 1640, a period known as the Great Migration, between 15,000 and 20,000 English settlers, mostly families, crossed the Atlantic. It was not fish or fur or even sassafras, a plant prized in the Old World as a supposed cure for syphilis, that drew them to distant Massachusetts Bay. Rather, it was King Charles I, whose hostility to both Parliament and the Puritans prompted many of his subjects to leave their homeland for New England. Though the news from that distant part of the world was not always encouraging, thousands of Puritans, it seemed, preferred to take their chances 3,000 miles away rather than face persecution at home.

Once they arrived in Newbury or Boston, the immigrants created a world whose rhythms were religious ones. In fact, religion permeated the whole culture: The names people bore, the thoughts they had, the books they read, the conversations they exchanged. Even their form of government (which granted citizenship only to church members) was colored by faith. Religion also left its imprint on the landscape: Wherever they settled, the immigrants were quick to establish a meetinghouse.

Built in 1681 by ship carpenters in Hingham, Massachusetts, this plain-looking meetinghouse, called the Old Ship Church, was the hub of the Protestant community.

The Mission of the Puritans

In leaving England for what would become New England, the Puritans were not seeking economic opportunity and security for themselves and their families. They were on a religious mission, or what later became known in Puritan circles as an "errand into the wilderness." Their goal was a complex one: to form a model Protestant society whose impact would be felt as much in the Old World as in the New. John Winthrop spelled out his hopes for the future of Puritanism in a rousing speech entitled "A Modell of Christian Charity" (1630):

Now the onely way to avoyde this shipwracke and to provide for our posterity is to followe the Counsell of Micah, to doe Justly, to love mercy, to walke humbly with our God, for this end, wee must be knitt together in this worke as one man, wee must entertain each other in brotherly Affeccion, wee must be willing to abridge our selves of our superfluities, for the supply of others necessities, wee must uphold a familiar Commerce together in all meekenes, gentlenes, patience and liberallity, we must delight in eache other, make others Condicions our owne, rejoyce together, mourne together, labour and suffer together, allwayes haveing before our eyes our Commission and Community in the worke, our Community as members of the same body, soe shall wee keepe the unitie of the spirit in the bond of peace, the Lord will be our God and delight to dwell upon us, as his owne people and will commaund a blessing upon us in all our wayes, soe that wee shall see much more of his wisdome power goodnes and truthe then formerly wee have been acquainted with, wee shall finde that the God of Israell is among us, when tenn of us shall be able to resist a thousand of our enemies, when hee shall make us a prayse and glory, that men shall say of succeeding plantacions: the lord make it like that of New England.

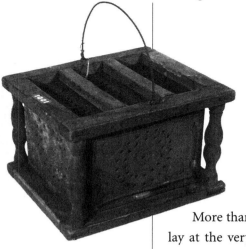

To ward off the chill, worshipers in colonial America often brought foot stoves, along with their Bibles, to Sunday services. Filled with glowing coals that emitted heat through the perforated metal sides, the "stoves" were the only source of comfort in unheated churches.

(Protestants fiercely avoided the use of the word *church.*) Duplicating the plain, unadorned structures they had known back home, Puritan settlers fashioned modest log or wooden houses of worship where altars, statues, and stained-glass windows were conspicuously absent. Any form of outward show and ornamentation, they believed, was vain and extravagant.

More than just houses of worship, their plain-looking meetinghouses lay at the very center of the Puritans' communal life: They were places where people gathered, stored their grain and gunpowder, and posted notices about everything from politics to prospective marriages. The meetinghouses' finest hour, though, took place on the Sabbath, or the Lord's Day, as the Puritans preferred to call it. Summoned to services by the ringing toot of a horn, the loud blowing of a conch shell, the beating of a drum, or the peal of a bell, the people would spend much of the day attending to their prayers and listening to a sermon that would last anywhere from two to five hours; anything less would simply not do. As a popular Protestant hymn, "New England's Sabbath Day," put it:

> New England's Sabbath Day
> Is heaven-like and pure
> When Israel walks the way
> Up to the Temple's door.
> The Time we tell
> When there to come
> By beat of drum
> Or sounding shell.

On the New England Sabbath day there was no work or play, no smoking or idle strolling, only what one member of the community called the "orderly and quiet going to and from the meeting." At first, during the early years of the colony, when church membership was at an all-time high, making attendance mandatory was unthinkable. After 1635, though, church attendance did become compulsory, and those who failed to take their seats in the sanctuary on the Sabbath were subject to a fine. So, too, were those who violated the Sabbath in other ways: As the colonists Aguila Chase and his wife, and Elizabeth Eddy of Plymouth, and a Captain Kemble of Boston would discover, even the mildest of infractions was punishable by law. In 1646, Mr. and Mrs. Chase were fined by the local authorities for gathering peas from their garden on the Sabbath. In 1652, Mistress Eddy was fined for doing her wash on that day. A worse fate befell Captain Kemble. Seen kissing his wife on the Sabbath, he was punished and placed in the local stocks for behavior said to be "lewd and unseemly."

As these examples suggest, not all the residents of the Massachusetts Bay Colony were saints. Even at religious services, they indulged in behavior that was far more human than saintly. Some worshipers, it seemed, were given to what one of their number called "sloth and sleepiness" when they should have been paying attention. Women at least had an advantage over their menfolk in this regard: hidden by their oversized bonnets, they could pretend to be listening when, in fact, they were dreaming. Their ministers, though, were not so easily deluded. One amiable cleric, a Mr. Whiting, subtly called his female congregants to task for their subterfuge: "Mr. Whiting doth pleasantlie say from ye pulpit hee doth seem to be preaching to stacks of straw." Other worshipers took advantage of the lull between morning and afternoon services to talk of this-worldly things. Instead of discussing the Bible, the sermon, or God's handiwork, they talked of their "farms, their crops of corn, their horses, their cows; or what's the price of this or that commodity," observed Increase Mather, a leading Puritan cleric, his antennae bristling at the indignity of it all. In another telling instance, a minister in

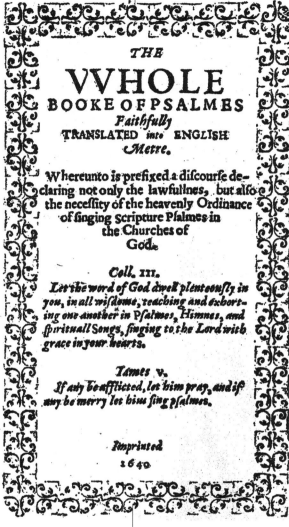

The Bay Psalm Book, a collection of Protestant hymns, was the first English-language book published in America. It was issued in 1640 by Stephen Daye in Cambridge, Massachusetts.

one of New England's coastal towns urged the locals to be more vigorous in their practice of religion, lest they "contradict the main end of planting this wilderness," an allusion to the Puritan mission. "You think you are preaching to the people at the Bay," replied one resident. But "our main end [is] to catch fish."

Whether catching fish, engaging in neighborly banter, or fervently at prayer, the Puritans, it seems, were actually a more diverse and varied lot than we have been led to believe. Some were very pious, others less so, and still others—especially those who came after 1660—had other things on their minds than salvation. By then, the arrival of a new kind of immigrant, the young and single soul in search of economic opportunity rather than freedom of religious expression, added to New England's human diversity. At the same time, the growing, disruptive presence of religious dissidents like Anne Hutchinson and Roger Williams complicated matters still further. Offering an alternative perspective on faith, they challenged the Puritan way.

Hutchinson, together with her husband and their 11 children, left England for Boston in 1634. A well-respected, well-born, deeply religious woman who emigrated for "conscience sake," she quickly reestablished herself in her new community. Hutchinson did "much good in our Town, in womans meetings at Childbirth-Travells, wherein shee was not only skillfull and helpfull but readily fell into good discourse with the women about their spiritual estates," related her good friend John Cotton. Before long, though, Hutchinson's "good discourse" about religion departed from the conventional wisdom. Setting forth "her own stuffe," she rejected the traditional Puritan belief that salvation was the consequence of piety and good works. Salvation, she believed, came only from God. An affront to the church and its ministers, Hutchinson's radical beliefs not only offered what she liked to think of as a "faire and easy way to heaven" but also threatened the religious ideals and practices that bound one Puritan to another. If what she said was true—and hundreds of Bostonians,

Drawing on their experiences in the Old World, colonists brought the idea of stocks to America. As punishment for such crimes as dancing and holding an unauthorized religious meeting, the transgressor's feet, and sometimes his head too, were locked between wooden planks for all passersby to see.

most of them women, were inclined to believe her—there was little point in going to church, submitting to one's husband, or conducting oneself with restraint and discipline. By Hutchinson's lights, all anyone had to do was to "waite for Christ to do all."

Clearly, this was a potentially explosive situation, one likely to expose the fault lines in Puritan society. Claiming that Hutchinson had created "disturbances, divisions and contentions . . . both in Church and State, and in families," the community's leaders moved against her. In 1636 she was tried in civil court, found guilty of "traducing [betraying] the ministers and their ministry," and banished. You are a troublesome spirit, she was told; a "woman not fit for our society." A few months after the civil court rendered its verdict, the church followed suit by excommunicating Hutchinson and publicly branding her a "heathen."

Hutchinson and her family went into exile in Rhode Island, the settlement established only a few years earlier by Roger Williams who, like Hutchinson, had been expelled from Massachusetts for his "new and dangerous opinions": belief in freedom of conscience and religious liberty. A haven for dissenters of all kinds, Rhode Island proved to be too close to the Massachusetts Bay Colony for Mistress Hutchinson's comfort, however. Fearing the long arm of the authorities, she moved as far away as she could, to the colony of New Amsterdam, in present-day Pelham, New York, where in September 1643 she was killed by Indians.

Hutchinson's death did not put an end to instances of religious dissent. In the years that followed, growing numbers of Quakers, Baptists, and members of other Protestant sects arrived in New England from the mother country. Determined to find a place for themselves as the Puritans had done decades

Massachusetts resident Anne Hutchinson (shown here in a romanticized 19th-century illustration) was adamant that the inner spirit, not the outward show of good works, defined Christians and led to salvation. Though vilified by her contemporaries for her views on God and religion, she is today remembered and even revered for expressing them.

earlier, they were instead made to feel unwelcome. The Quakers had an especially rough time of it: When not banished altogether from the Massachusetts Bay Colony, whose leaders refused to countenance the idea that Quakers were truly Christians, they were subjected to whippings and imprisonment and had their literature confiscated.

Little wonder, then, that the Quakers, or Friends, as they called themselves, eventually forsook New England for Pennsylvania, a colony established in 1681 by William Penn as a "holy experiment," a place where the Quakers might freely and fully practice their religion and transmit their beliefs to the next generation. Hundreds of Quaker families, like that of Welshman John Bevan, his wife, and their four children, were among them. The news that their "esteemed Friend" William Penn had secured a patent, or official permission from King Charles II to establish, for a "Province in America called Pennsylvania" was especially pleasing to Mrs. Bevan, a devout Quaker. "My wife had a great inclination to go thither," wrote her husband. She thought it "might be a good place to train up children amongst a sober people and to prevent the corruption of them here [in Wales] by the loose behavior of youths and the bad example of too many of riper years." Mr. Bevan, though along in years and not keen at the prospect of starting all over again, eventually conceded to his wife's wishes. Her aim, he later explained, was an "upright one," and "on account of the children, I was willing to weigh the matter in a true balance." Sometime in 1683, the entire family migrated to Merion, Pennsylvania, where they prospered: "Our children married with our consent, and they had several children, and the aim intended by my wife was in good measure answered."

Like the Bevans, many other religious dissenters found Pennsylvania and the adjacent colonies of Delaware, New York, and New Jersey—the so-called "middle colonies"—to be the answer to their prayers. A far cry from New England, where practicing other forms of religion was a crime, the middle colonies attracted a wide variety of Protestant settlers—Anglicans, Baptists, Huguenots, Lutherans, Mennonites, Moravians, Quakers, and Presbyterians—as well as non-Protestant groups such as Jews and

Quakers suffered persecution in America as well as England. They practiced a distinctive form of community worship, praying in silence until one of the members decided the time was right to stand up and speak. This scene of a Quaker meeting dates from the end of the 18th century.

Catholics. All were drawn by the prospect of both religious and economic freedom. Even the small colony of New York, as Thomas Dongan, its Catholic governor, pointed out in 1687, numbered "Singing Quakers; Ranting Quakers; Sabbatarians; Antisabbatarians; Some Anabaptists; some Independents; some Jews," and many folks who were "none at all."

The situation farther south, in the Carolinas and Maryland, was much like that in the middle colonies: Throughout the 17th century, religious variety went hand in hand with religious indifference. In North Carolina, recalled the Quaker leader George Fox in 1672, settlers had "little or no religion, for they came and sat down in the meeting smoking their pipes." Irreligious or perhaps merely ignorant of Quaker ways, the Carolina colonists nevertheless welcomed the Protestant sect into their midst, as they did the French Protestants called Huguenots who settled in Charleston, South Carolina, in the 1680s. Much of the time, though, Carolinians displayed little active interest in Christianity.

Fleeing religious persecution at home, a small band of French Protestants called Huguenots, led by Captian Jean Ribaud, arrived at the St. Johns River in Florida in 1563 and then continued up the coast to South Carolina. They were succeeded more than a century later by several larger groups.

Religion fared only slightly better in Maryland. Set up early in the 17th century as an avowedly Catholic colony, Maryland failed at first to attract a sufficient number of Catholic settlers. Other religious groups, including Protestants and Quakers, filled the vacuum, but their numbers and resources were far too limited to make much of an impact. More common by far were settlers with little interest in matters religious, many of them young indentured servants inclined to think more about this world than the next. It is against this background that, in 1649, Maryland passed the "Act Concerning Religion," a piece of legislation which, in hopes of keeping friction to a minimum, prohibited settlers from hurling religious insults at one another. To label someone a "Heretic, schismatic, Idolator, puritan, Independent, Presbiterian, popish priest, or Jesuite," among other names, was no longer permissible, insisted the Maryland authorities. Highlighting the number of different religious groups that had taken to calling Maryland home, the "Act Concerning Religion" ultimately was as much a plea for a strong and civil Christian presence in Maryland as it was a plea for tolerance.

The range of religious (and for that matter nonreligious) expression that now became increasingly characteristic of the colonies was a reflection both of the New World's size and spaciousness and of its changing immigration patterns. By the end of the 17th century and the opening years of the 18th, as news of the New World spread, settlers no longer hailed exclusively from England or identified solely with Puritanism. Thousands upon thousands now came from Scotland and Ireland, France and Switzerland, the German Rhineland and Silesia, "carry[ing] with them their forms, worship, rules and decency," wrote J. Hector St. John de Crèvecoeur, whose *Letters from an American Farmer,* published in 1782, offered a detailed account of life in the colonies; his comments about religion were particularly astute. Upon arriving in the New World, he said, the newcomers "immediately erect a temple, and there worship the Divinity agreeably to their own peculiar ideas. Nobody disturbs them." What is more, "if they are peaceable subjects, and are industrious, what is it to their neighbors how and in what manner they think fit to address their prayers to the Supreme Being?"

Nowhere was this more true than in Pennsylvania, home throughout the 18th century to a stunning array of German-speaking religious communities, from the Anabaptists to the Moravians, the Schwenkfelders, the Seventh Day German Baptist Brethren, and the Dunkers, who owed their name to their insistence on immersing (or dunking) the entire body during baptism instead of submitting to a gentle sprinkling of holy water. Mainstream Protestant denominations such as the Lutherans and the Reformed church also found Pennsylvania congenial. On the eve of the American Revolution, that colony alone could boast more than 200 Lutheran and German Reformed churches. The greatest flurry of religious activity, however, occurred within the camp of the smaller and more radical Protestant element.

The Anabaptists, for instance, had long been harassed and persecuted in Europe for their beliefs. Anabaptists rejected infant baptism and the power of the state, among other things. Two offshoots of the Anabaptists,

The writings of J. Hector St. John de Crèvecoeur, a nobleman farmer from New York, did much to publicize the freedom of religion in 18th-century America. He characterized the new nation as "the most perfect society existing in the world."

the Amish and the Mennonites, sought shelter and salvation in Pennsylvania during the late 17th and early 18th centuries. Determined to live simple lives—what one of their number called a life of "Christian humility"—they kept to themselves and shunned contact with the outside world. The Amish and the Mennonites also spoke German, or *deutsch*, rather than English, which prompted subsequent generations to call them the Pennsylvania Dutch. Some say this phrase is simply a corruption of the word *deutsch*, while others point out that it was the way English speakers of the time referred to those who hailed from the lower and middle Rhineland.

Hard-working and industrious, the Amish and the Mennonites prospered as farmers. For all their economic success, though, they not only rejected the temptations of secular society but proudly and purposefully stood apart from it, especially in the manner of their dress. Items that made up the fashionable wardrobe of the 18th century, such as lace, feathers, and wigs, were rejected for their worldliness. Instead, the members of these two communities proclaimed their collective disdain for,

The Amish preferred to educate their children in their religion and ways in unadorned church schools segregated from the world at large. This photo was taken in the Amish community of Hinkletown, Pennsylvania, in 1942.

and renunciation of, the material world by dressing simply and modestly in plain clothes, as they called them, referring to the somber, dark palette of their wardrobes; the old-fashioned, broad-brimmed hats of the men and the gauzy white caps worn by the women. The Amish, in fact, went even further than their Mennonite cousins in rejecting the material world, by regarding all newfangled things, from buttons and suspenders to modern farm implements, as suspect. Even today, more than 200 years later, the Amish of Lancaster County, a community of some 20,000 people, keep these traditions intact and alive.

Young Amish girls wear dark-colored dresses and bonnets that defy time and changing fashions. At the heart of Amish life is a belief in a simple life.

The Amish and the Mennonites were by no means the only radical Protestant sects to flourish in Pennsylvania during the 18th century. "You can hardly imagine how many different groups you can find here," wrote Christopher Schultz in 1768 to friends back home in Germany, noting how the funeral of a respected local personality brought together followers of Kaspar Schwenkfeld like himself, with Mennonites, Lutherans, and an occasional Catholic. "We are all going to and fro like fish in water." Among those who seemed to multiply like fish in the sea were the Moravians and the Seventh Day German Baptist Brethren.

An evangelical Protestant church whose origins dated back to the 15th century, the Moravians, or Renewed Unity of Brethren, as they called themselves, believed that Christian faith had more to do with the play of emotion than the rule of reason. They also believed that the best way to practice their faith was to form communities of like-minded people who not only worshiped together but lived and worked side by side. Separating from the world at large, Moravians saw themselves as members of a new kind of family, the "family of God." Those within the fold called each other brother and sister; everyone else was designated a *fremde,* the German word for stranger.

Moravian beliefs and practices did not sit well with more traditionally minded Protestants in Europe who, early in the 18th century, began to make life so unpleasant for the community that several hundred of the Brethren decided to leave the Old World for the New. Emigrating as a group in the 1730s, they settled in Georgia, whose governor, James Oglethorpe, had invited them to establish a settlement and a missionary school for Native Americans. But when asked to bear arms to fight against the Spanish, an act that ran counter to their deeply held pacifism, the Moravians elected to leave. The community then relocated up north, in Pennsylvania, where its members formed two new settlements, each proudly bearing a biblical name: one was called Bethlehem, the other Nazareth. Later still, when a vast tract of uninhabited land was made available in the piedmont section of North Carolina ("a region that has perhaps been seldom visited since the creation of the world," wrote August Gottlieb Spangenburg, the Moravians' leader in the New World), dozens of Moravians ventured into the southern frontier. By the 1760s they had established a number of settlements in and around Salem, North Carolina, on land they liked to think had been "reserved by the Lord" just for them.

"I set my staff forward in God's name and wander cheerfully in a strange land," declared a member of a Protestant sect from Salzburg, Austria, as he set off for the New World early in the 18th century. The so-called "Salzburg-ers" found a warm welcome in Georgia.

Living apart from other settlers and speaking German rather than English, the Brethren sought to enclose themselves and their offspring in holiness. "We don't want extraordinary Privileges, if only we can live together as Brethren, without interfering with others and without being disturbed by them; and if only we can keep our Children from being hurt by wicked Examples and our young people from following the foolish and sinful ways of the world," Spangenburg explained. An elaborate system of do's and don'ts, of rules and regulations, including the strict segregation of the sexes, ensured the community's special character. "All Brethren must rise with the first bell in the morning; they must be punctual, orderly and clean; they may not smoke tobacco in the house and must not be in any of the rooms without lights being on," stipulated the rules for the single men of the community, all of whom lived together under one roof. Even their bedtime was prescribed. According to a regulation issued in 1744, the Single Brethren "must all retire at the usual time (10:30 P.M.) unless special permission has been granted." The major moments in a Moravian's life, no less than the minor ones like bedtime, were also closely regulated. When to marry and whom, how to earn one's keep, and where to live were decisions made by the community's leaders, not its individual members.

Moravians also made no distinction between the sacred and the profane; they thought that one infused the other, from the prayers that began and ended each day to work in the fields, tanneries, and kitchens. A popular hymn, one of thousands written or collected by the Moravians, gave

The little town of Bethlehem in the Lehigh River Valley in Pennsylvania was settled by a group of Moravians who moved north from Georgia in 1735.

voice to the way religion suffused even the most humble of household tasks such as spinning:

> Know ye, sisters, in this way
> Is your work a Blessing.
> If for Jesus's sake you spin,
> Toiling without ceasing.
> Spin and weave;
> Compelled by love;
> Sew and wash in fervor
> And the Saviour's grace and love
> Make you glad forever.

For all their religious fervor, the Brethren did not entirely forsake the outside world. Unlike the Amish or the Mennonites, for instance, who firmly turned their backs on secular society, the Moravians were not averse to limited forms of interaction with *fremden*, provided, of course, that they were sanctioned by the community's elders. Most exchanges were economic ones: Owning and operating stores and taverns or exporting pottery, leather goods, and foodstuffs to bustling port cities like Charleston, South Carolina, brought the Moravians into the world and in frequent contact with others. Though at first all commercial transactions were frowned upon (according to one communal saying, "Sin adheres to [commerce] in the same way as a nail does to the wall"), they enabled the Moravians to be self sufficient and to sustain their own unique way of life. As a practical means to a holy end, trade was tolerated.

Little by little, though, this 18th-century version of a "city on a hill" began to give way under both the subtle and not-so-subtle pressures of Americanization. For one thing, the German language lost ground to English, though not before generating a certain degree of controversy between the older generation and the new. Young people today, complained George Bahnson, a Moravian from North Carolina, in 1864, don't understand German; the older people in turn "prefer the German so decidedly as hardly to admit English on any solemn occasion, funerals excepted." For another, those born in America took less and less kindly to the community's stringent economic and social controls than did their parents and grandparents. Where the latter accepted rules and regulations as a matter of course, their descendants did not. Growing up in the aftermath of the American Revolution, they questioned and eventually challenged curbs placed on their individual freedom. Meanwhile, the distance that the Moravians had put between themselves and the outside world began to shrink with the steady development of the frontier during the late 18th and early 19th centuries. Keeping the world at bay was no longer possible. Unable to resist the forces of change, the Renewed Unity of Brethren eventually gave up its identity as a self-contained religious community and became a church, one of many that dotted the American landscape on the eve of the Civil War.

In their heyday, the Moravians probably had some contact with the members of the mystical community known as Ephrata, home to the Seventh Day German Baptist Brethren. Under the charismatic leadership of its Ger-

The Brethren and Sisters of Ephrata, near Lancaster, Pennsylvania, created some of the most beautiful illuminated hymn books and other manuscripts in colonial America, as this illustration of an Ephrata Sister shows.

man-born founder, Conrad Beissel, the members of this sect, many of them former Mennonites or Quakers, completely renounced the workaday world and its conventions. Forming their own self-enclosed settlement in 1730, some 15 miles outside of Lancaster, Pennsylvania, the members dressed in monklike garb, practiced celibacy, and celebrated poverty. Some among them even chose to live a cloistered life, leaving behind their husbands and children.

Ephrata was not without its pleasures, however, from its pumpernickel bread, known throughout Lancaster County for its tastiness, to its glorious music, which some likened to the sound of angels. One eyewitness, the Reverend Jacob Duche of Philadelphia, having had the opportunity of hearing the Ephrata community in song, was transfixed by the experience. Clad all in white, their faces drawn and solemn, the singers (largely women) sang simple but richly harmonious tunes that "thrilled to the very soul," he recalled. "I almost began to think myself in the world of spirits, and the objects before me were ethereal. In short, the impression this scene made upon my mind continued strong for many days, and I believe, will never be wholly obliterated."

But then, the Sisters as well as the Brothers of Ephrata were angelic in nature too. During the American Revolution they devotedly took care of those wounded in battle, even though warfare ran counter to their pacifist principles. As one soldier later recalled, "I came upon this people by accident, but I left them in regret. . . . Until I entered the walls of Ephrata, I had no idea of pure and practical Christianity. Not that I was ignorant of the forms, of even the doctrines of religion. I knew it in theory before; I saw it in practice then." By that point, though, the community was on its last legs: Internal squabbling, coupled with the aging of its members and an inability to recruit new ones, soon led to its demise. By the early 19th century, all that remained of Ephrata was its crumbling buildings.

Even as sectarian communities like Ephrata and Salem dwindled away, the established, mainline Protestant churches grew stronger. During the 19th century, new waves of immigrants from Germany and Scandinavia added to the ranks of Protestant believers in the New World, bringing the precepts and practices of the Lutheran church with them to the American heartland. In search of greater economic opportunities than those available at home, where poor harvests and local famines made life extremely difficult, more than 2 million Germans came to the United States during the first half of the 19th century. Divided by religion—nearly half of all German immigrants were Protestants, a third were Catholics, and the remainder included freethinkers as well as Jews—they shared a common destination: the Midwest, especially Missouri and Wisconsin. "Nowhere but in the West," a popular 1856 guidebook told them encouragingly, "can the immigrant so quickly find employment and abundant sources of income, which, with hard work, sobriety and thrift will secure independence for him in so short a period of time, even if he arrives penniless."

Some German immigrants, like the 600 members of a Lutheran congregation in the German state of Saxony that resettled as a group in Perry

County, Missouri, 100 miles west of St. Louis, were well prepared for life in the New World. Along with their clothes and their cutlery, they came bearing what one of their number described as a "large theological library, a pipe organ, a collection of church music, instruments for a band, three church bells and the sacred vestments." Others, however, like the immigrants whose presence transformed Milwaukee into one of the nation's most German of cities, had to start from scratch, building Protestant churches and religious schools from the ground up. Milwaukee, wrote John Kerler, Jr., who settled there in 1850, is a place where the "German language and German ways are bold enough to take a foothold. You'll find inns, beer cellars, billiard and bowling alleys, as well as beer, something you do not find much of in this country." Eventually, visitors could also find a number of congregations like Holy St. Paul's, Holy Trinity, or Grace Church, where German was the language of prayer. From humble beginnings in which members met in one another's homes, these churches grew into imposing stone edifices, complete with bell towers with a powerfully sounding set of bells. Rung twice a day during the week as well as on Sundays, the church bells added a distinctive aural quality to Protestantism in the Midwest, making its presence not only felt but heard.

As German immigrants by the thousands made their way to the New World, they were joined by Scandinavians, first from Norway and then from Sweden. Large-scale emigration from Norway did not begin in earnest until the early 1820s, when a small group of Norwegian Quakers, sailing aboard the aptly-named sloop the *Restoration,* sought freedom from persecution in a country where Lutheranism was the sole national

This 19th-century drawing illustrates a collection of communion vessels on an altar of a Lutheran church in York, Pennsylvania. They include a silver box for the Host, or communion wafer, and a gilded chalice that held the wine.

religion. In the decades that followed, though, most Norwegians emigrated largely for economic rather than religious reasons: At home, too many people were forced to eke out a living on too few acres of land. Learning of America's natural bounty, Norwegian farmers and their families made haste to emigrate. Between 1836 and 1850, more than 18,000 Norwegians left for the New World. Over the next decade, their numbers swelled to nearly 60,000.

Swedish immigration, in turn, was largely a post–Civil War phenomenon. In the years prior to that conflict, approximately 15,000 Swedes, including a number of Methodist and Mormon families as well as the members of a radical sect called the Janssonists, left their homeland in search of religious freedom. As in Norway, Sweden tolerated only one form of religious expression, Lutheranism, making life hard for those who followed a different belief. Later, after the war, between 1868 and 1873, and again between 1880 and 1893, nearly 600,000 Swedes emigrated, this time largely for economic reasons. The continuing absence at home of available land to farm, coupled with growing unemployment in the lumber and iron industries, prompted both farmhands and factory workers to try their luck in the New World.

Most Norwegians and Swedes gravitated toward the Upper Midwest, peppering the landscape from Lake Michigan to the Dakotas with their settlements. Many became farmers, as they had been back home, while others, settling in Chicago and Minneapolis, worked in trades. Often, the choice of a home or an occupation was prompted by something prospective immigrants might have read in a letter or guidebook or in the Scandinavian press, which widely publicized news of the New World. "In America you associate with good and kindly people. Everyone has the freedom to practice the teaching and religion he prefers," wrote Gjest G. Hovland in 1835 from his new home in Wisconsin to his family back in Norway. When you take into account the friendliness of the people and the fertility of the land, surely "this is Canaan," he declared optimistically, referring to the Old Testament name for the Promised Land. "People here have just as good opportunities to worship God as in Norway."

Like the biblical Canaan, its latter-day American counterpart was not without its difficulties. The first wave of Scandinavian settlers had to endure harsh frontier conditions, much illness, brutally cold winters, and excessively hot summers. Compounding these difficulties was the small number of Lutheran pastors to tend to the immigrants' spiritual needs; only a handful accompanied their parishioners as they made their way from one part of the world to another. In the absence of an established religious presence, settlers had to make do, calling on one another to conduct services, using a roughhewn wooden table for communion and a beer glass for a chalice. Without a regular pastor or even a modest house of worship to call their own (it would take years before settlers could afford to build one), some even took to worshiping elsewhere. "Several of us who have lived here long enough to know English fairly well do not feel the lack of [a pastor]. We go to the Episcopal, or Protestant, church which agrees with the Lutheran in practically everything," confessed one Wisconsin resident in 1845. "In fact, we are so happy with the Episcopal church that we don't intend to write to the Norwegian Lutheran church to send us a clergyman. No! There are very few things that we can import from our Old Norway which could be of benefit to us, and least of all Norwegian [church] officials."

Immigrant farmers from Sweden, mostly Lutherans, brought their farming skills to the New World. They settled mostly in the Midwest, where the scenery reminded them of their homeland.

On the sweeping Great
Plains of South Dakota,
three churches—one
Lutheran, another Baptist,
and a third Catholic—
formed a snug, safe haven.

Meanwhile, the few Lutheran church leaders who did emigrate along with their flocks often faced considerable discord. Any pastor who comes over to America, wrote one, finds that a "battle of controversy" awaits him. "Confused by silly notions of liberty," Norwegians in the New World "take it into their hands to reorganize the church community," challenging religious authority at every turn. Religious leaders from the Church of Sweden fared no better than their Norwegian counterparts. Helplessly, they watched as their people worshiped elsewhere or not at all. It was simply impossible to organize a religious congregation, lamented pastor Lars Paul Esbjorn, his patience worn thin by repeated failure. The Swedes in America, he observed, "wish to know nothing of piety." Neither were the pious themselves strangers to conflict. Time and again throughout the 19th and early 20th centuries, their ranks were split between those who favored the use of Norwegian or Swedish during the church service and those who preferred English; between those who clamored for more cere-mony and greater religious authority and those who argued for less.

Despite a steady succession of quarrels and disappointments, the Lutheran Church took root in America, becoming one of the nation's leading Protestant denominations. It may have taken a different turn than it had in Norway, Sweden, and southern Germany, where church and state went hand in hand, but it flourished all the same, filling the newcomers' need for community as well as for faith. As Norwegian journalist, Ole Munch Raeder, sagely declared in 1847 as he traveled throughout the Upper Midwest observing the ties that bound Scandinavians to their faith: "Even if the situation is by no means what it was among the Puritan set-tlers in New England 200 years ago, when a church was the first thing to be provided for, nevertheless spiritual needs do assert themselves even out here in the West, as soon as the first severe struggle with nature is over." Religion, he was glad to see, continued to appeal to most Scandinavians. "Many a person who never has experienced the influence of religion in a thickly populated, civilized country, learns to appreciate, out here in his loneliness, how deep an influence religion exerts upon the soul of a man."

Protestantism, then, not only left its mark on colonial society; its imprint on America of the 19th century was just as visible and just as deep. Following the tradition laid down in the 1600s by William Bradford and his small band of Pilgrims, hundreds of different Protestant commu-nities since then have dreamed of security and stability amid the "free aire of the new world." In time, as the past receded and the future beckoned, these Protestant groups set in motion a new and equally promising tradi-tion of religious pluralism and acceptance. It is not that the Pilgrims or the Mennonites or the members of the Norwegian Evangelical Lutheran Church of America set out to establish a commonwealth where religious diversity was the rule; it just happened, a consequence of immigration, an accident of timing. But once it did, religious pluralism—in theory and in practice—was well on its way to becoming the law of the land.

Chapter 2

The Land of Sanctuary: The Catholic Immigrant Experience

O n a bright sunny day in late May of 1879, Catholics from across the country gathered in New York City to dedicate St. Patrick's Cathedral. Built at a cost of more than $2 million (at the time a staggering amount of money), the "greatest Temple in the New World dedicated to God" took more than 21 years to construct and was still not finished at the time of its dedication: it had no steeples. Even so, the spirits of those present soared that May morning. Thousands of Catholic faithful clogged Fifth Avenue, eager to show their support, while just as many took their seats inside the beautifully proportioned Gothic cathedral, where they spent the better part of the day. There was so much to do and say, apparently, that the dedication ceremony lasted for nearly five hours (the sermon alone ran to one hour and 40 minutes), making it clear to all that American Catholicism had finally come of age. By then, Catholicism had so many followers, from the "adobe Catholics" of the Southwest to the "lace-curtain" Irish Catholics of the Northeast, that it could proudly lay claim to being the single largest religious body in the entire United States. Majestic houses of worship like St. Patrick's Cathedral in New York and St. Brigid's Church in San Francisco prominently lined the nation's main streets while an elaborate network of con-

Each year on Easter Sunday, the holiest day in the Christian calendar, St. Patrick's Cathedral in New York City is a gathering place for crowds taking part in the Easter parade.

vents, seminaries, and parochial schools produced enough nuns and priests, as well as educated lay members, to fill and sustain them. In addition, a cocoon of institutions and events—clubs, hospitals, professional societies, and parish fairs—enveloped the Catholic immigrant's daily life, adding to its fullness.

A mighty alternative to Protestantism, which it denounced, Catholicism more than held its own in 19th-century America. The early history of the Catholic Church in the New World, though, was anything but promising. Catholic missionaries, seeking to convert the Indians of Canada, the Caribbean, and the Southwest, were present in the New World as early as the 15th century. The first organized community of lay Catholics did not take root, however, until the 1630s when Lord Baltimore, or George Calvert, as he was called by friends and family, received a charter from the king of England to establish a colony in what is today the state of Maryland. Devoted more to profit making than to God, the colony was initially intended as a commercial venture. But practical considerations, especially the overriding need to attract settlers and investors regardless of their religious background, gave rise to a concern for religious toleration and quality, prompting Lord Calvert to hail his colony as a "land of sanctuary." This arrangement was a fragile one, though, as Calvert and his son and heir, Cecil, were well aware.

Even before Catholics arrived in the New World—in fact, while still on board the ships that would transport them across the sea—they were cautioned to keep a low profile and avoid antagonizing their Protestant fellow travelers. A bloody century of hostility between the two had taught Catholics to be wary. "All acts of Roman Catholique [sic] Religion should be done as privately as possible," Cecil Calvert suggested, adding it would be a

Catholics were active in founding missions along the California coast and the Southwest. Early in the 18th century priests at the San Antonio de Valera mission in San Antonio, Texas, sought to convert local Indians to Christianity. In April 1883 the state of Texas bought the mission, which included the church known as the Alamo, from the Catholic Church.

good idea if Catholics remained "silent" about and kept away from discussions concerning "matters of religion."

The Calverts' cautionary Catholicism dominated the American Catholic experience for quite some time. A holdover imported from Europe, cautionary Catholicism was kept alive by the harsh realities of life in the New World, where practicing Catholics and their institutions were few and far between. As late as 1785, Catholics comprised considerably less than 1 percent of the total population. Outnumbered by and swallowed up in the vastness of the New World, some 23,000 Catholics had to rely on only 34 priests and a handful of modest brick and wood chapels to minister to their souls. As a result, most Catholics in America tended to practice their religion largely at home, where women, rather than priests, kept the faith. The women of a household shouldered all responsibility for organizing prayer services, baptizing the young, and seeing to their religious education.

The fact that Catholics experienced a great deal of outright hostility and discrimination at the hands of America's Protestant majority who looked down on them also encouraged the development of a low-key, private form of Catholic religious expression. Subjected to a raft of discriminatory measures that remained on the books well into the 1780s (and, in some states, much beyond that date), Catholics could not practice law, hold elective office, or own property. We are "almost reduced to a level with our Negroes, not even having the privilege of Voting," wrote one aggrieved American Catholic on the eve of the Revolution. We are "deprived of all the advantages promised our Ancestors." No wonder, then, that for much of the 17th and 18th centuries American Catholicism was anything but vibrant.

By the 1850s, the situation had changed markedly. No longer a small, scattered, virtually invisible religious community, American Catholics had become a well-populated, highly urban, much-noticed religious enterprise. Once a lonely outpost, the Catholic community could now proudly point to 3 million adherents, 2,385 churches, and 2,235 priests. Immigration had turned the situation around. Without the steady influx of millions of Irish, then German, Italian, Czech, and Polish immigrants who came to North America beginning in the 1820s and concluding a century later, in search of security and freedom, Catholicism would have remained a slender presence in the New World. As it happened, the good fortune of the church was completely and inextricably bound up with that of the American immigrant experience. Immigrants swelled the number of the faithful and imprinted Catholicism on the religious landscape. Bringing with them and developing an alternative form of worship, and with it alternative notions of community, Catholics tested and ultimately enlarged the limits of America's commitment to religious pluralism.

Some observers, especially those within the church hierarchy or establishment, attributed the success of the "American Church" to divine intervention. Those of a more practical mind, however, attributed it to more earthly causes, to what one donor called the "children's pennies, the widow's mite, and the laborer's contribution of money and time and brawn." At first, many of those pennies came from the pockets of Irish immigrants. Taking advantage of the increasingly affordable fares offered by the Cunard Line on transatlantic steamships that ran directly and often from Londonderry and Liverpool to Boston, young Irish men and

As early as 1629, Irish immigrants began arriving on America's shores to escape worsening oppression by the English. By the first half of the 19th century, the numbers had grown to 100,000 annually, as shipload after shipload arrived in the Northeast.

women by the droves fled their increasingly inhospitable homeland. For much of the 1820s and 1830s, Ireland was racked by devastating economic and demographic crises ranging from overpopulation to unemployment. To make matters worse, the devastation of the potato crop, the mainstay of the Irish diet, left millions with very little to eat. Famine, which ravaged the country between 1846 and 1853, further cut short the promise of a secure, healthy future. This event alone prompted even more Irish men and women—by some estimates as many as a million—to pull up stakes. Scores of single Irish men and women settled in large urban

areas like New York, Philadelphia, and Boston, where they could easily find work as laborers and laundresses. In the city, they also sought—and found—the consolations of companionship. The familiar sounds and sensations, liturgy, and rituals of the church brought them together, reminding them of the past. They also shepherded the immigrants toward a new future in which their local or parish church became the focus of a resolutely American Catholic identity.

The failure of Ireland's potato crop in 1845 and the ensuing famine that continued for decades, swelled the ranks of Irish emigrants. Unlike their predecessors, who had chosen farming, the new immigrants crowded into cities such as New York, Boston, Philadelphia, and Baltimore.

In the decades that followed, their numbers were strengthened by the arrival of nearly a million German Catholics. Like the Irish before them, they too left behind a country weakened by a potato blight and facing economic uncertainty. Political unrest as well as frequent outbursts of anti-Catholic expression throughout the 1870s prompted by the efforts of Otto von Bismarck, the German chancellor, to subject his nation's Roman Catholic Church to his control, added to the combustible mix, making emigration an increasingly attractive option. Many German Catholic immigrants, especially those who had been small shopkeepers and artisans, headed for America's urban areas, transforming cities like Milwaukee and St. Louis into *Kleine Deutschland* (Little Germany). Others, especially those accustomed to tilling the soil, headed even farther into the

German American Catholics, like other immigrant groups, set up societies to take care of their own. This invitation to a meeting of the German Society of New Orleans symbolizes what the New World had to offer— riches on the one hand and power on the other.

interior, where they could farm. Wherever they settled, German Catholics made sure to build houses of worship whose language, choral music, and interior decor were similar to those they had left behind.

Whether they lived in the city or on a farm, most Catholic immigrants preferred to worship in their mother tongue and among their own kind. At home in their native language, be it Gaelic or German, they also strongly preferred that their priests be of the same ethnic background as themselves. Acting on these preferences, immigrants from Ireland and Germany, and later still others from Italy and Poland, profoundly changed the nature of the Catholic Church in the United States by creating a new religious phenomenon: the ethnic church. "The Irish," wrote the Reverend Jeremiah Cummings in 1847, "find it difficult to discard their affection for everything that concerns Old Hibernia. . . . the Germans stay on their own and do not want to have anything to do with the Irish," while the small community of French-speaking Catholics, centered around Detroit, would like to "dress up" the Catholic Church *"à la française"* (in the French manner). Unable and unwilling to resolve their differences, the Irish ended up worshiping among the Irish, the Germans among other Germans, and the French with their *frères* and *soeurs* (brothers and sisters). The result was a system of national parishes, each with its own set of churches, priests, parochial schools, and literature. In this parallel universe, Irish Catholic youngsters would learn about the principles of their faith by reading an abridged version of *Dr. Butler's Catechism*, a concise compendium of Catholic precepts, which sold for a mere two cents, while German youngsters would learn exactly the same principles by reading the *Kleine Katechismus*, a text so popular among German-American Catholics of the 19th century that it went through 38 editions by 1889.

Though divided by language, Irish and German Catholics were one in their disdain for the public school. Unlike most American boys and girls, whose time in the classroom was split between public school, where they learned secular subjects, and Sunday school, where they learned about religion, Catholic boys and girls went to parochial school, where they were taught both. Centered in the parish, from which it took its name, the parochial school was believed to be the most effective way to transmit the faith to the next generation. At the same time, it was also seen as a very effective way to limit the Catholic boys' and girls' encounters with the outside world, encounters uniformly believed to be hostile to Catholic values. An alternative to the public school whose "benefits," declared New York's Archbishop John Hughes, "are not for us," parochial

In the fall of 1911 the city of St. Peter, Minnesota, played host to a convention of German Catholics. As the proud conventioneers marched down the broad, unpaved main street, carrying American flags, the townspeople gathered to watch.

Going to Parochial School

Americans have often viewed the parochial school with suspicion, claiming, among other things, that it robbed American boys and girls of a solid, well-rounded education. But, as this excerpt from writer Mary McCarthy's celebrated 1956 memoir, Memories of a Catholic Girlhood, *suggests, the parochial school could also liberate the imagination and free the spirits of at least some of its students.*

Looking back, I see that it was religion that saved me. Our ugly church and parochial school provided me with my only aesthetic outlet, in the words of the Mass and the litanies of the old Latin hymns, in the Easter lilies around the altar, rosaries, ornamented prayerbooks, votive lamps, holy cards stamped in gold and decorated with floral wreaths and a saint's picture. This side of Catholicism, much of it cheapened and debased by mass production, was for me, nevertheless the equivalent of Gothic cathedrals and illuminated manuscripts and mystery plays. I threw myself into it with ardor, this sensuous life, and when I was not dreaming that I was going to marry the pretender to the throne of France and win back his crown with him, I was dreaming of being a Carmelite nun, cloistered and penitential. I was also much attracted by an order for fallen women called the Magdalens. A desire to excel governed all my thoughts, and this was quickened, if possible, by the parochial-school methods of education, which were based on the competitive principle. Everything was a contest. . . .

I stood at the head of my class and I was also the best runner and the best performer on the turning poles in the schoolyard, I was the best actress and elocutionist and the second most devout, being surpassed in this by a blind boy with a face like a saint, who sat in front of me and whom I loved, his name, which sounds rather like a Polish saint's name, was John Klosick. No doubt, the standards of the school were not very high, and they gave me a false sense of myself, I have never excelled at athletics elsewhere. Nor have I been devout again. When I left the competitive atmosphere of the parochial school, my religion withered on the stalk.

schools, staffed by nuns and priests, took root in Catholic communities across the country. Some, like the high-toned Academy of the Sacred Heart in New York City, instructed Catholic girls in the principles of their faith as well as in the "habits of politeness, industry, neatness and order." Others, like St. Stephen's in Minneapolis, recalled writer Mary McCarthy, one of its former students, emphasized "civics and conformity."

Not all Catholics favored the system of national parishes; in fact, the largely Irish leadership of the church sought to discourage it, urging the faithful to think of themselves as members in full of an American Catholic church rather than a hyphenated one. But proudly ethnic Catholics such as the Reverend P. M. Abbelen, a leader of Milwaukee's German Catholic community, turned a deaf ear to these entreaties, bringing matters to a head. In 1886, Abbelen wrote to the Vatican, seeking its help in placing German churches "on an equal footing" with those administered and peopled by Irish Catholics or, as he called them, the "American" Catholics.

In short order, controversy erupted between the two groups of Catholics, creating what John Gilmary Shea, editor of *Catholic News,* called bitter feelings of "dissension [and] jealousy." The controversy, in part, grew out of the desire of each ethnic church to guard itself against interference from the Vatican; then again, it was also rooted in fear that the ethnic church might resist becoming a truly American institution. Church leaders pleaded for unity, urging Irish Catholics and German Catholics, Polish Catholics and French Catholics to think of themselves as *American* Catholics. It no longer matters where we come from, exhorted Baltimore's James Cardinal Gibbons, a great champion of a true-blue American Catholicism, as he presided in 1891 over the investiture, or installation, of a German archbishop in Milwaukee. It is not important if we were born in America or became citizens at a later date, he argued. Let all of us "glory in the title of American citizen." After all, "this is America," agreed the editors of the *Catholic Review.* "Within the American Church there must be no nationalism."

But "nationalistic" feelings were hard to overcome. For many Catholic immigrants and their children, the language, symbols, sensibilities, and customs of the Old World—even its architecture—were not easily disentangled from their faith. For the German immigrants of the 19th century as well as those that followed them in the 20th—the Italians, Cubans, and Haitians—Catholicism and ethnic identity went hand in hand. Persisting instead of disappearing, as so many predicted it would, ethnicity challenged the Catholic Church in America to make room for everyone.

At least once a year, thousands of Italian Americans were able to put away their "vaunted American ways" and be "Italian through and through," by participating in a religious street festival or *feste*, a tradition imported from the Old World to the New, explained Anna C. Ruddy, author of a popular early 20th-century novel about the Italian immigrant experience. Luigi, the hero of Ruddy's novel, was among them. "The joy of it!" exclaimed Luigi, thrilled to be a "part—an important part—of a great pageant. The joy of it!" Taking to the streets, ablaze with brightly colored lights and electric with excitement, Luigi and other residents of Little Italy, the generic name given to the urban neighborhoods peopled by immigrants from Salerno, Sicily, and Basilicata, gathered on the sidewalk where "impromptu restaurants" offered "Italian dainties of every description," from cannoli to macaroni. Dressed in their Sunday best (Luigi proudly sported "new clothes, from head to foot"), they munched, strolled, and chatted freely, prompting one delighted spectator to write in 1901 that never had he seen a "happier crowd" of people.

It was a devout crowd as well, come to pay its respects to those who embodied their religious tradition and sustained their faith. Mingling religion and merrymaking, the crowd watched in amazement and delight as several pairs of unseen hands lifted two young girls, dressed as angels, over the railings of a fire escape and suspended them in midair before an outdoor altar featuring a statue of Christ on the Cross. After offering their prayers, the angels ascended heavenward, dropping flowers en route and winning the applause, reported one eyewitness, of "Sicilians, Basilicatians and Anglo-Saxons." At other times, the Madonna was the object of devotion and affection. As early as the 1880s and continuing well into the 1940s, residents of East Harlem in New York, for example, would fill the streets in celebration of the *feste della Madonna di Monte Carmelo* the

feast of the Madonna of Mount Carmel, a celebration that "went on and on" for nearly an entire week, recalled an eyewitness.

The crowd-pleasing festivities, which featured marching brass bands and dazzling displays of fireworks, began with an elaborate procession through the streets of East Harlem, home to one of the largest Italian communities in the United States. Placing a statue of their beloved Madonna on a float bedecked with ribbons and flowers, the entire community—girls from the Children of Mary Society, all dressed in white; boys from the Holy Name Society in their somber Sunday suits; barefoot penitents bringing up the rear—would march alongside, following the Madonna as she made her way under the steel trestles of the noisy elevated subway, the Third Avenue "El," and up and down the narrow, mean streets of East Harlem. Some carried a single taper while others held aloft a multi-tiered altar of candles resembling a wedding cake. Some shouted messages of thanks to the Madonna or tried to touch her while others expressed their

Italian Americans were especially fond of street festivals honoring religious figures. Several times a year, entire Italian neighborhoods, like this one in Chicago in 1947, took to the streets in public celebration of their faith.

devotion by pinning dollar bills onto a large banner which, in bright, bold letters, spelled out "Congregazione del Monte Carmelo."

As the procession wound to a close, crowds of celebrants proceeded upstairs, into the main sanctuary of the Church of Mount Carmel, on East 115th Street, where an imposing, life-size statue of the Madonna greeted them. Italian Catholics, usually relegated to the basement, the *chiesa inferiore* (lower church), delighted in the opportunity to make the main sanctuary their own, if only once a year. Patiently, for hours on end, they waited in line so that everyone might have a chance to celebrate an upstairs mass in the Madonna's honor. At its conclusion, the devout streamed down the aisle to the altar, bearing hard-earned gifts of clothing, food, jewelry, and money. "Every offer represents a sorrowful tale of great sufferings, of unexpected joys and of eternal gratitude," noted one church publication. "Each heart is enclosed in that offer. Tight in their trembling hands it represents the fruit of their labour, and for many it probably represents their daily sacrifice." Clutching a scapular, a small piece of cloth that bore the Madonna's image—a gift from their priests—celebrants then exited the church, hopeful that she had given them her blessing and with it sanctioned their lives in the New World.

The Madonna of Mount Carmel had come to the United States along with her people in the 1880s. Like Europeans everywhere, "stirred" by what one student of migration named Broughton Brandenburg poetically called the "tide of unrest," Italians—especially those living in the southern part of Italy—faced steadily mounting crises, from unemployment to overpopulation. As matters worsened, more and more young Italians left for America in search of work and the chance to live a fuller life. Between 1880 and 1890, more than 30,000 Italians a year—mostly men—arrived in the New World; a decade later, their ranks swelled to more than 65,000 immigrants annually, making Italians the single largest ethnic group of the time to enter the country.

Some Italians, recruited by U.S. business organizations, processed sugarcane on Louisiana plantations; others, signed up by their own countrymen known as *padroni* or labor bosses, paved roads, dug ditches, and, through their labor, built the urban Northeast from the ground up.

Although men predominated among Italian immigrants, women came too. Clutching straw baskets and makeshift luggage, and holding entry cards between their teeth, they were ready to make a new life for themselves.

Leaving their families behind, most Italian immigrants planned on staying in the United States temporarily, only until they had earned enough money to be able to return to their hometowns in Polla and Valledolmo and comfortably live out the rest of their lives. That they would return was "understood, of course," recalled one immigrant matter-of-factly. And most did; unlike their eastern European Jewish counterparts, the vast majority of Italian immigrants had no intention of staying in the United States for more than a few years.

Still, an estimated 1.5 million Italians ended up calling America home. For one reason or another—they found a good job or fell in love or both—they chose to reside permanently in Buffalo, Chicago, Philadelphia, New Orleans, San Francisco, and New York. Settling in narrow, cramped tenements and two-family houses that came to hold two or three times that number of people, Italians lived together, worked together, ate together, and relaxed in the company of their own kind. Eager to keep alive ties to the Old World, they also fashioned dozens of hometown or regional societies—East Harlem alone boasted 64 of them—where they might sip an espresso, play cards, exchange news from the Old Country and, in things large and small, take care of one another. Members also took care to honor their patron saints, often naming their societies after them. "The Italian feels safer when he pays homage to the patron saint of his hometown or village," explained a member of one such group, adding that "without [its] guardianship . . . life would be next to impossible."

Though they came from different towns and regions and honored different saints, Italian immigrants shared a common Catholicism. Unlike the German immigrants, for example, whose numbers included not just Catholics but Protestants of different denominations as well as Jews, all Italians claimed Catholicism as their religion. This bound them together, unifying them into a community whose compass turned on faith as well as geography. The churches they erected, like the Church of Our Lady of Mount Carmel, the very first Italian-built church in New York, reinforced the connection between the two. Founded by former residents of Polla, this church, with its handsome campanile, or bell tower, a familiar landmark of Italian villages everywhere, welcomed worshipers who hailed from other towns and villages, creating a broad, expansive sense of community.

No matter how familiar or accommodating the church and its priests might be, they did not lie at the center of Italian immigrant life. Nor, for that matter, did the parochial school, which educated only a small percentage of the community's sons and daughters. The radius of Italian immigrant culture was the home, its presiding spirit the Italian mother; together with the family that inhabited it, the home was just as sacred to Italians as the sanctuary, and perhaps even more so. Not the most avid of churchgoers—even in the Old Country many did not attend on a regular basis—Italians lived day to day in a world rich in religious symbolism and ritual, one peopled by household saints.

Religion was so intertwined with family life that it was hard to tell where one began and the other left off. For one thing, the decor of the home was just like that found at church: The scent and sight of dozens of illuminated candles filled the dining room; delicately colored holy cards, imported at first, then made in America, hung on the walls while painted wood shrines to the Madonna and other saints adorned the bedroom and even the backyard. Watching over the household, the saint's statue,

We obtain
from
the Good God
as much
as we hope
from him

ST. TERESA
OF THE
CHILD JESUS

An intimate declaration of faith, this small handmade prayer book, decorated with an image of Saint Teresa, reinforced ties between home and church.

observed photographer Jacob Riis at the turn of the century, was a domestic as well as public "rallying point." For Italian immigrants, the saint means "home and kindred, neighborly friendship in a strange land and the old communal ties." Domestic rituals, especially those having to do with food, were also sanctified. "Eating was the sacrament of the home, and the Sunday meal was more important to the immigrants than regular attendance at mass," commented one Italian American. You could skip mass now and then, but you could not skip Sunday dinner, "You had to be there." In addition to Sundays spent in the bosom of the family, baptisms, first communions, and weddings—occasions at once religious and familial—enlivened the rhythms of Italian daily life.

But was it religion? And was it Catholic? Initially, many American Catholic leaders were not too sure. Referring darkly to a growing "Italian problem" within the church, they believed that Italian immigrants suffered from a "peculiar kind of spiritual condition," one that placed too great a premium on the "luxuries of religion" and too little on its "great truths." "Their religion, what there is of it, is exterior," sniffed one critic. When compared with the formal, liturgical "church Catholicism" espoused by the American Catholic establishment, a Catholicism presided over by priests and bishops, the Catholicism practiced by Italian immigrants and given shape by women not only seemed to be of an entirely different order but appeared to be an entirely different religion. In many respects it was. An example of what historians call "popular religion," Italian Catholicism drew on and reflected the people's way of being Catholic. Informal, lively, and always within reach (the saints, after all, "belonged to the people, not to the church," observed Riis), Italian Catholicism took root in the streets and kitchens of its followers rather than in the wooden pews of the churches or behind a school desk at St. Vincent's. No wonder, then, that the American Catholic establishment looked down its nose at Italian Catholics, consigning them along with their statues and candles to the basement rather than the main sanctuary, and frowning at their *festes*. "We were always looked upon as though we were doing something wrong," recalled one Italian American, bitter at the memory. The Catholic Church in America "didn't accept [us] at all."

But that would change. With the passage of time, the Catholicism practiced by Italian Americans became less and less distinctively Italian and more and more American. Where Italian immigrants had delighted in pinning dollar bills on Madonnas and dancing in the streets, their American-born children and grandchildren preferred the discreet collection envelope and more subdued, decorous forms of religious expression. As a result, noisy, boisterous street festivals like that of the Madonna of 115th Street suffered a decline in popularity. From crowds in the hundreds of thousands, attendance dropped to approximately 20,000 by the 1950s, inspiring Father Zema, an Italian-American priest who championed assimilation, or blending in, to note proudly that Italian Catholics were well on their way to becoming American Catholics. Their "marked growth in Catholic living," he wrote, "is becoming more and more impressive."

Even so, Italian Catholics profoundly affected the way Americans understood religious commitment. In its easy embrace of the sacred and the profane, the street and the sanctuary, the public and the private, the religious experience of the Italian immigrant community transformed

modern America's notion of religion. Religion, they suggested, was a lived, day-to-day affair, not something reserved for Sundays and an occasional holiday. As social worker Ada Eliot put it at the turn of the 20th century, those of us whose "religion wears a somber hue and to whom duty is a stern lawgiver" have a lot to learn from the Italians. They show us how to "mingle joy and gaiety with worship."

Like the Italians before them, subsequent waves of Catholic immigrants to the United States also expanded the repertoire of rituals associated with Catholicism, testing the receptivity of both the church and the nation to change. The *quinceañera,* a coming-of-age ceremony popular among Hispanic Catholics, is a case in point.

"If you're a teen-age girl in the Cuban-American suburbs west of Miami, fifteen is more than a birthday, it is a major life decision," observed *The New York Times* in 1995 in an article describing the elaborate, floor-length, white gowns young Cuban-American girls wear to their *quinceañera,* a celebration of their passage into both womanhood and Catholicism. The same could be said of teenage Puerto Rican girls in the Bronx and their Mexican-American counterparts in Phoenix, where of late one local church, Immaculate Heart, performs more *quinceañeras*

The celebration of the *quinceañera*, marking the coming of age of 15-year-old Latina girls, usually begins with a thanksgiving Mass attended by maids of honor and chamberlains as well as close family and friends.

than weddings. Part debutante ball, part religious service (a special mass is usually said), the ceremony has grown steadily in popularity over the years. In some parts of the country, it has become a multimillion-dollar business in which caterers, party planners, and dress designers participate with relish; there is even a magazine, *Solo Para Fiestas (Just for Parties)*, devoted to the subject. Much like the bar mitzvah, a once-modest Jewish rite of passage that became enormously popular—and increasingly more elaborate—the *quinceañera*, a Mexican tradition, has taken hold throughout the entire Latino Catholic world in the United States, transcending geography and history as well as class. "It is an old-fashioned event," conceded the mother of one celebrant whose *quinceañera* was held at a posh Phoenix country club, "but I love it."

The growth of the *quinceañera* reflects that of the Latino or Hispanic community, today one of the nation's fastest-growing populations as well as Catholic America's single largest constituency. Made up of disparate groups—of Mexicans, Puerto Ricans, Dominicans, and Cubans—most (though not all) of whom share a common Catholicism as well as the same language, its roots extend as far back as the 16th century, when large numbers of Mexican Indians were converted to Catholicism by the Spanish. Since then, *católicos* from south of the Rio Grande, together with those from Santo Domingo; Ponce, Puerto Rico; and Havana have come to call America home.

Mexicans first began to enter the United States in large numbers in the early 1900s, in search of steady, better-paying jobs. At the time, little stood in the way of crossing the border. "All one had to do," recalled Conrado Mendoza, "was to get on the electric trolley or streetcar and cross over to the United States, and no one told you anything." Settling at first in southern Arizona and South Texas, where they worked in the mines or on the railroads, Mexicans like Mendoza subsequently moved to California where, thanks to innovations in the use of irrigation, the Golden State was becoming one of the nation's largest producers of fruits and vegetables. In need of agricultural laborers, especially after the U.S. government passed a series of laws in the early 1920s restricting immigration from Europe and Asia, California attracted an estimated 1.5 million Mexicans by 1930.

While Mexicans were transforming Los Angeles into Little Mexico, thousands of Puerto Ricans were also on the move. During the first two decades of the 20th century, an average of 250 to 1,000 emigrated annually to the mainland in search of better economic opportunity. Not until after World War I, though, did this population movement assume large-scale proportions, giving rise to what is now known as the Great Migration. As conditions worsened on the island following a devastating hurricane in 1932, in the years between 1946 and 1964 more than half a million Puerto Ricans availed themselves of increasingly accessible and affordable airline fares to leave home. Most chose to settle in New York where, like so many immigrants before them, they encountered an inhospitable city and a wary church.

And then, just as the Great Migration was winding down, a new chapter in the history of U.S. immigration

Migrant workers, like this young cotton picker in California's San Joaquin Valley in 1939, formed the nucleus of the Mexican-American community in the Southwest. They came in search of work and freedom from political turmoil at home, but for many the work was grueling and the pay meager.

began to unfold. More than 700,000 Cubans, fleeing the political turmoil and economic hardship wrought by Fidel Castro's 1959 socialist revolution, perilously made their way across the Atlantic to Florida. Most took up residence in Miami. Before long that city claimed nearly as many Cuban residents as Havana itself.

Despite differences of geography and history, the first generation of Latino immigrants was bound together by a common approach to religion. Although not everyone espoused Catholicism (once in America, a goodly number were drawn to evangelical Protestantism), those who did practiced a form of Catholicism centered more in the home than the church, a Catholicism the Mexican-American writer Richard Rodriguez calls "home Catholicism." A natural, organic part of daily life, Catholicism, he writes in his autobiography, *Hunger of Memory,* "shaped my whole day. It framed my experience of eating and sleeping and washing; it named the season and the hour." Catholicism "filled my life."

While the Rodriguez family went faithfully to church—"they were deeply pious," their son explains—many other Latino households did not. Some, keeping to a long, Old World tradition of both anticlericalism and irregular church attendance, continued to stay away. Others simply found the American Catholic Church not to their liking—"too gringo"— and kept their distance. Relegated to the basement, for *las misas de sotanos* (basement masses), where their "loud" singing and "fiesta" style of prayer would not disturb the established, English-speaking parishioners, they found fellowship someplace else. Still others, like Manuel, a 16-year-old Mexican immigrant, discovered a new way to spend Sundays. My friends and I "quit going to church because we wanted to play baseball on Sunday mornings," he explained.

In all other respects, though, Latino Catholics maintained strong ties to their faith. As a Texas priest associated with the San Benito parish observed in 1925, referring to the Mexican immigrants he knew, "They have a great religious mind in their own way. . . . They do not despise the religion, they do not use blasphemies in their language, they respect the *padrecito* [an affectionate term for father or priest] and most of them have religious pictures in their homes."

In home after home in the barrio, or neighborhood, brightly colored religious pictures of saints like the Mexican Virgin, *Nuestra Señora de Guadalupe,* or *La Ermita de la Caridad,* Our Lady of Charity, the patron saint of Cuba, did indeed take center stage, watching over the faithful from their perches in the living room or bedroom. Often "holy pictures" shared space with *altarcitos,* or home altars, whose assemblages of religious icons and personal objects blurred the boundaries between the public and private faces of religion. Extremely popular within the Mexican-American community, home altars made the divine presence visual and real. *Santos,* hand-carved wooden statues of the saints or of scenes based on biblical themes, did much the same thing.

In Puerto Rican households, where they typically inhabited a home altar or populated a shelf, *santos* not only provided a tangible link with

Among Mexican Catholic families, church and home were closely intertwined. Many, especially in the 1940s, created sacred spaces in a part of the house with elaborate displays of religious images and family mementos.

the Old Country but were a source of comfort and visual pleasure as well. He used to fall asleep at night, recalls Ramon Estrada-Vega, a Puerto Rican immigrant, "watching the shadows of the saints dancing on the walls and ceiling. The candles on the altar made the shadows flicker and dance—they looked so big!" Yard shrines also loomed large in Latino neighborhoods. Hundreds of them, ranging in size from two to ten feet in height, graced the urban landscape. While no two were exactly alike, most usually contained a small statue of the Madonna or a revered saint encased in a structure made of brick, cement, stone, and glass; flowers (plastic or freshly cut), candles, crucifixes, and other devotional objects rested at its base. Facing the street, the yard shrine made public one's commitment to faith.

Both within and beyond the barrio, Latino immigrants were also bound together by ongoing ties to their country of origin, or what is known in Puerto Rican circles as *va y ven* (back and forth). Where so many other immigrants remained entirely cut off from their homelands, those from Puerto Rico and Mexico were able to, and often did, return home, if only for a brief visit, because proximity and politics were in their favor.

Cuban immigrants, to be sure, faced an entirely different situation: They could not go back home. Feeling displaced and in exile, they harbored an intense desire to return to Cuba ("Next Christmas in Havana!") and, since the 1960s, have worked diligently and passionately behind the scenes to topple Castro's socialist regime. In the meantime, pilgrimage sites like Miami's waterfront shrine to Our Lady of Charity, a new sacred center in the heart of the city, help Cubans sustain a sense of connectedness to their homeland. Built by the local Cuban community with the full support of the diocese of Miami and consecrated in 1973, the shrine is as much a national symbol as a religious one. "Cuba and the Virgin are the same," related one frequent visitor who, together with thousands of other weekly visitors, comes to pray for herself, her family and, above all, for Cuba. Said another, "All is connected for me, *patria* (homeland) and the Virgin." Even those whose ties to Catholicism have frayed seek out Our Lady of Charity, explaining that in America immigrants like themselves simply "need more help."

When it came to adjusting to life in the United States, thousands of Latino immigrants, especially those from Cuba, turned to Santeria as well as Catholicism. Though a new development in this country, Santeria has a long history in Cuba, dating as far back as the 16th century. Blending Spanish Catholicism with Yoruba traditions brought to the Caribbean by West African slaves, Santeria, which literally means the "worship of the saints," fuses the identity of Yoruba *orishas* or deities with Catholic *santos* or saints and the sacraments with animal sacrifice. A mix of religious traditions and practices, it maintains its own network of male priests, known as *babaloos*, who make use of stones, plants, potions, and animals to communicate with the spirits. With its familiar deities and age-old rituals, Santeria provides an enduring connection with the Old World while offering a more intimate alternative to New World Catholicism, whose size and scale some immigrants find unfamiliar and intimidating.

For much of its history, Santeria was practiced in secret. In 20th-century America, though, its followers sought to worship openly and freely. Here, in the New World, we can become as "mainstream as everyone else,"

Representing the biblical Magi (wise men) from the East who came to honor the Christ child in Bethlehem, the Feast of the Three Kings on January 6 represents the end of the Christmas celebration among Puerto Rican Catholics in New York's barrio.

The Cuban Day parade up New York's Fifth Avenue is a celebration of Cuban heritage and religion.

insisted Ernesto Pichardo, founder of the Church of Lukumi Babalu Aye, in which the ceremonial sacrifice of chickens, roosters, pigeons, and goats is routine. "We really have nothing to hide, so why are we hiding?" Determined to hide no longer, Pichardo took steps in 1987 to build a Santeria church and community center in the Florida city of Hialeah. But city officials, alarmed at the prospect, quickly passed a series of ordinances outlawing animal sacrifices, in effect forcing the church to shut down, at least publicly. "We welcome any legitimate church that comes into the city," explained its mayor, Raul Martinez. "But the laws of the land must be abided by. And the laws of the state of Florida prohibit the sacrifice of animals, whether it be for sports, or religious practices, whatever."

Pichardo and his 70,000 followers, however, did not agree. With the help of lawyers from the American Civil Liberties Union, they contested the city's right to ban animal sacrifices. "It degrades the First Amendment," charged Pichardo as he took Hialeah's officials to court. "Here we are taking 70,000 people in South Florida and making them outlaws because they use animals for religious purposes." At first, local courts ruled in favor of the city. Eventually, though, the case reached the U.S. Supreme Court where, in 1993, it unanimously ruled in favor of the Santeria church. The ban on ritual animal sacrifice violated the religious freedom of those who practice Santeria, declared the highest court in the land in *The Church of Lukumi* v. *Hialeah*.

The action taken by the Hialeah authorities violated the First Amendment's guarantee of the free exercise of religion, said the U.S. Supreme Court, and, as a result, it overturned the ban on sacrifices. "Our review," stated the justices, "confirms that the laws in question were enacted by officials who did not understand, failed to perceive, or chose to ignore the fact that their official actions violated the nation's essential commitment to religious freedom. . . . Although the practice of animal sacrifice may seem abhorrent to some, the religious beliefs need not be acceptable, logical, consistent, or comprehensible to others in order to merit First Amendment protection. . . . Given the historical association between animal sacrifice and religious worship, petitioners' assertion that animal sacrifice is an integral part of their religion cannot be deemed bizarre or incredible. . . . We must consider petitioners' First Amendment claim."

Pichardo and his followers were jubilant at the verdict. The U.S. Supreme Court's ruling, they told *The New York Times,* would surely improve their religion's image. In the meantime, "Eleqba (referring to the Santeria God of Destiny) is hungry," said Irma Gonzalez, a member of the Church of Lukumi. "He needs to be fed his roosters to strengthen him."

Like Santeria, Vodou (or Voodoo), an Afro-Haitian religion that believes as much in otherworldly spirits as in real-life saints, has also recently found a home for itself in urban America. During the 1970s, Haitian immigrants, fleeing economic turmoil and widespread political repression at home, emigrated to the United States in large numbers, bringing the rituals and traditions of Vodou, their folk religion, with them. A blend of West African beliefs and practices with those of French Catholicism, Vodou, which means deity or spirit, has gradually become a part of America's religious landscape. In the storefronts, church basements and

A drummer from Haiti summons the spirits of his African ancestors while his companion marks the beat on an iron bell in a Vodou ceremony in Brooklyn, New York.

private homes of this country's estimated 800,000 Haitian immigrants and their American-born children, Vodou priests and priestesses like Mama Lola, a celebrated Brooklyn, New York, *manbo,* or intermediary between the spirit world and this one, call on the spirits of Ezili, Legala, and other Vodou divinities to heal, comfort, and sustain one another.

Back home, 85 percent of Haitians, it was said, were Catholic, 15 percent were Protestant, and 100 percent "serve the Vodou spirits." Here, in the New World, as the Haitian celebration of Our Lady of Mount Carmel, the *Fête du Notre Dame du Mont Carmel,* vividly demonstrates, the situation is not much different: Catholicism and Vodou continue to be seen and experienced as part of a religious whole. In what has become the single largest annual religious gathering of Haitians in North America, the fête both draws upon and revitalizes the century-old American Catholic tradition of making a pilgrimage to the Church of Our Lady of Mount Carmel in East Harlem. With a round-the-clock mass, elaborate feasting, and lively street processions punctuated by fireworks, it is similar in many respects to the *festa* first established at the turn of the century by Italian Catholic immigrants. The fête differs, though, in its language—French and Creole rather than Italian are now heard on the streets of East Harlem during the two-day celebration—and in its integration of Vodou rituals into the festivities. Celebrants dress in light blue, the color of Ezili, or white, a color that, in the "ritual vocabulary of Vodou," explains anthropologist Elizabeth McAlister, is the "symbol of spiritual newness." They leave offerings to the spirits, place heaps of petitions in Creole before one of the Madonnas in the church whose skin is painted a shade darker than that of other statues, and pray to Our Lady of Mount Carmel and Ezili at the same time. For Haitian immigrants, Catholicism and Vodou are all of a piece or, as Madame Luc, a devout, churchgoing Haitian Catholic, explains: I believe deeply in Catholicism, but I "think in Vodou."

In each instance, whether communing with the spirits, making wooden *santos*, or celebrating a daughter's *quinceañera*, Latino Catholic immigrants have not only changed the rhythms and sensibilities of the church. They have also enlarged the meaning of popular religion, attesting to its continued hold on millions of Catholics across the country. At the same time, though, Latino Catholics have kept alive a tradition that is perhaps as old as the American Catholic Church itself: the tradition of diversity. Taking their place alongside the Irish, German, Italian, and Polish Catholic immigrants of earlier generations, they have seen to it that the church continues to remain open to and embrace Catholics of many different backgrounds, from those who speak Spanish rather than English to those who pray to the sounds of maracas rather than organ music. Perhaps more diverse at the beginning of the 21st century than it has been at any previous point in its history, the American Catholic Church continues, as it has in the past, to make the nation's newest settlers feel a part of something larger than themselves. "There's tension at home, there's tension at work, there's even tension on the way to work," observed Frankie Vazquez, a deacon of St. Martin of Tours, a Catholic church in the Bronx whose parishioners, once Irish and Italians, are now largely Latinos. "At least church should be a place of peace."

Chapter 3

In the Promised Land: The Jewish Immigrant Experience

O n or about 11 o'clock on a muggy July morning in 1902, traffic in lower Manhattan ground to a halt. Tens of thousands of New Yorkers—perhaps as many as 50,000; the police were not sure—had taken to the streets to participate in the funeral of Jacob Joseph, their chief rabbi. The entire Lower East Side, recalled an eyewitness, referring to the city's immigrant Jewish neighborhood, "was streaming with people, hurrying and scurrying" to get a glimpse of the coffin. Even the fire escapes were packed with men, women, and children closely watching what journalist Abraham Cahan called the "largest Jewish procession of its kind ever held on American soil." Ever so slowly, the procession wound its way up one gray, scowling street and down another, accompanied by an honor guard of 300 young boys and what *The New York Times* described as a "cavalcade of mourners."

Like the late rabbi, a transplant from Vilna, Lithuania, most of the mourners were themselves relative newcomers. They were among the 675,000 eastern European Jews who had emigrated to the United States between 1881 and 1900, transforming the country and themselves in the process. Mostly young, single, relatively uneducated and unskilled, these "unfinished people," as Ruth Gay, the daughter of two such immigrants,

Congregants in Dorch- ester, Massachusetts, gather in May 1939 to mark Shavuot, an ancient festival that celebrates the giving of the Torah to the Israelites in the Sinai. Typically, this event takes place 50 days after the first day of Passover.

describes them, left their families in Bialystok, Kiev, and Warsaw with the intention of eventually calling New York, Boston, Philadelphia, Chicago, and even St. Joseph, Missouri, their home. Some were devout Jews who prayed three times a day and scrupulously kept the Sabbath, the dietary laws, and the many other rituals that characterize the practice of traditional Judaism. Others had not set foot in a *shul* (synagogue) since landing in America and had no intention of visiting one anytime soon. And still others clung halfheartedly to a few familiar domestic traditions, continuing to keep the Jewish dietary laws or to light the Friday night candles that ushered in the Sabbath but retaining little else besides. Every one of them, however, came to this country determined to put the past behind and start afresh. Having read in newspapers and books of the New World, its fast-paced cities and democratic culture, eastern European Jews fervently believed that America was better. And safer.

By the late 19th century, amid a grinding cycle of poverty and intensifying anti-Jewish prejudice, eastern European Jews had soured on the Old World. Dwindling economic opportunities coupled with a steadily mounting number of unprovoked pogroms, or physical attacks, pointed to a bleak future. Torn between futility and despair, growing numbers of eastern European Jews reluctantly conceded the hopelessness of their situation and made plans to leave at the earliest opportunity. Or, as the Russian Hebrew poet Y. L. Gordon put it in 1883 in the wake of a physically and emotionally devastating pogrom:

> Arise, let us go, since we've no loving mother's home
> To seek refuge in and peace
> No mother, no home of hers to dwell in
> Let us find another inn. . . .
> Arise, let us go! Where the light of freedom
> Shines on all men and brightens all souls. . . .

Though some stayed, hoping a revolution might change things (it did not), approximately two-thirds of the entire Jewish population of eastern Europe eventually packed its feather quilts, Yiddish and Hebrew books, and brass candlesticks in makeshift cardboard suitcases and heavy metal trunks and left for the ancient Holy Land or the modern "Promised

Jewish immigrants were both fearful and optimistic about what awaited them in America. This group of men arrived in Galveston, Texas, in the summer of 1907 as part of a project to help Jews settle west of the Mississippi.

Land" of America. In its scope and intensity, this migration, explained one of its sons, the distinguished literary critic Irving Howe, resembled a "collective utopian experiment," a group effort at establishing a better life for all. "When your barely literate Jew, with his few scraps of Hebrew and his kitchen Yiddish, ran away from pogroms to sweat and sometimes starve in New York and Chicago slums, he was indeed thinking of himself—but he was thinking of himself *as a Jew,* which is different from simply thinking about himself. It was characteristic of Jewish life that a sense of collective fate should become implanted in almost every Jew's personal experience."

That "collective fate" weighed heavily, indeed, on Rabbi Jacob Joseph's slender shoulders. Invited by a group of self-appointed Jewish lay leaders to be what the English-language press mistakenly called a "sort of bishop" (Jews have rabbis, not bishops) to guide, nurture, and represent America's growing Jewish immigrant community, the gentle, unsophisticated scholar arrived in New York in 1888 to take up his post. From the moment a huge crowd of well-wishers gathered at the Hoboken, New Jersey, pier that

July to accord him a hero's welcome, much was made of Jacob Joseph and his high office.

Even the English-language press, sensing a story, covered the historic arrival of America's very first chief rabbi. One such newspaper, the *Commercial Advertiser*, reported as follows: "The East Side has the greatest Yiddish wedding bands, the greatest synagogue singers, the greatest Yiddish actors, one of the leading Hebrew poets; and in persuading Rabbi Jacob Joseph to come and preside over their religious life, they congratulated themselves" for having obtained the very best rabbi. "The people of the East Side," the paper continued, a bit unkindly, "are quick to pick up American ideas, and one of the first things they learn is to reach out for everything that's 'the biggest in the world.'" With their newly acquired zeal, "the people of the East Side" lionized their latest acquisition, the "Chief Rabbi of New York and Environs." They flocked to his sermons (which were standing-room only), eagerly sought out his counsel, and actively enlisted his support for their projects.

Little by little, though, the community began to lose its taste for its imported rabbi; his old-fashioned ways no longer appealed to them. Rabbi Jacob Joseph "was the same but his listeners had changed," explained the Yiddish journalist Abraham Cahan, who published a moving eulogy of the "Hebrew patriarch" in a popular English-language magazine shortly after his death. They were in "hourly contact" with modern culture while he remained a "man of the 3rd century," deeply steeped in ancient Jewish texts. They "looked down upon" their rabbi, and took to calling him "green"—a term, Cahan hastened to explain, "that is applied . . . to everything that is not up to the American standard."

All too aware of his fading reputation, Rabbi Joseph took steps to win it back. Straining to speak English, a language he did not know, instead of Yiddish, a language he knew intimately, he sought to involve himself directly in his congregants' lives and in the often messy world of politics and business. But being "neither a man of affairs nor a fighter," the chief rabbi stumbled. "And all this, so far from tending to bridge over the gulf between him and his flock, only seemed to accentuate the unnaturalness of his position," remarked Cahan sadly, noting how the rabbi's audiences gradually thinned out, his sermons became few and far between, and sightings of the chief rabbi more and more infrequent. Retreating from public life, Rabbi Jacob Joseph ultimately fell ill and languished until he died on July 28, 1902, at the age of 59.

A day later, when the people of the East Side lined the streets to bestow on Rabbi Jacob Joseph the kind of honor they had denied him during his lifetime, it is no wonder that "a sigh of sorrow and of something akin to remorse" could be heard throughout the neighborhood. Mourning the good rabbi, the Lower East Side also mourned the old ways of the past.

In time, the memory of Rabbi Jacob Joseph and his failed tenure as New York's first and only chief rabbi faded away. The Lower East Side and other Jewish immigrant neighborhoods like South Philadelphia and the West Side of Chicago, however, grew dramatically, thanks to the influx of an additional 1,346,000 eastern European Jews between 1901 and 1914.

In the crowded outdoor markets of Chicago's Maxwell Street, immigrants encountered the bounty of America in markets much like those in their homelands. The overhead sign, written in Yiddish, denotes a fish market.

Why you do not have to travel to Europe any more to see a real ghetto, related *The New York Times* at the turn of the century, adding a new word to its readers' vocabulary: the European term for the segregated living conditions under which Jews were once forced to live. Ghettoes can now be found right here in America. "No walls shut in this Ghetto, but once within the Jewish quarter, one is as conscious of having entered a distinct section of the city as one would be if the passage had been through massive portals."

Their "distinct" address was not the only thing that set Jewish immigrants apart from others; Judaism, their distinctive religious tradition and culture, also distinguished them. Neither Catholics, like their Italian neighbors down the block, nor Protestants, like their public school teachers, the Jews stood outside the Christian framework that held the nation together. Even so, they fervently believed in America and worked hard to ensure that its promise of religious liberty might extend to them as well.

To be sure, the ghetto was no Garden of Eden. Filled with what social reformer Minnie Louis called the "Three D's—Dirt, Discomfort and Disease," it was also dark, dank, and unpleasant. "You cannot even faintly comprehend what the situation is," one concerned citizen, Cyrus Sulzberger, told a well-heeled audience of social workers in 1902, alluding to the Lower East Side. "The immigrants don't live with sunlight, trees or fresh air. They live—no, they don't live. They are packed away like raisins in layers. . . . That is barely a metaphor—that is almost the literal truth. Imagine putting 300,000 people into one square mile. Imagine what that means."

The residents of America's so-called "great ghettoes," though cramped physically, were by no means cramped culturally, intellectually, or spiritually. On the contrary. Freed from the yoke of the past, they threw themselves with remarkable energy and vigor into the creation of a new and lively Jewish community. Like mushrooms, mutual aid societies sprang up everywhere. Cushioning the transition from the Old World to the New, they provided a warm and congenial setting in which immigrants from the same geographical area in Europe could share together in the immigrant experience. Under the protective social cover of, say, the Adler Young Men's Independent Association Number One or the First

Lemberger Gentlemen's and Ladies' Support and Sick and Death Benefit Society—virtually all these organizations boasted highfalutin' names on the theory that the more ornate, the better—newcomers to the United States ordered the chaos of immigrant life. They would turn to their "society" for help, for unemployment insurance, medical benefits, and interest-free loans; for conversation over a cup of strong Russian tea and the much-anticipated opportunity to dress up and attend an annual ball.

Some mutual aid societies doubled as religious congregations, renting a modest little room in which to hold Sabbath and holiday services. Hundreds of these "storefront synagogues" dotted Jewish neighborhoods, with their handwritten Yiddish signs, swinging loosely from a metal chain, announcing the daily schedule of prayers. Inside, services were noisy, informal, and, for some tastes, perhaps a bit too matter-of-fact. Throughout, a "subway rush hour spirit" prevails, complained one disgruntled worshiper. "Pandemonium reigns," said another. With its foreign customs and language, this kind of synagogue, hotly declared a third, "is American by geographical location only."

In ghettos such as the Lower East Side in New York, immigrant families had little choice but to live in small, dingy apartments. If they were unable to pay the rent, the landlord was more than happy to evict them because another family would always be waiting in the wings.

From their earliest days in the United States, Jewish settlers eagerly helped the less fortunate among them. This "modern" Jewish Hospital in Cincinnati opened its doors in 1901 and even boasted a state-of-the art children's ward.

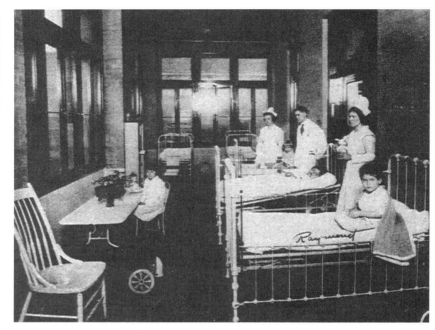

Those with a hankering for a traditional synagogue that was American in spirit as well as in geography had no need to despair. Such synagogues did exist, though not in great number, or not yet anyway. The Eldridge Street Synagogue, to use its English name, was one of them. Dedicated in 1887, it was the very first synagogue as well as the largest built by eastern European Jewish immigrants on the Lower East Side. "The building looks quite imposing, standing in the neighborhood it does," reported the *American Israelite* newspaper, adding that the sanctuary was "distinguished by an elegant simplicity." In their top hats and frock coats, their Sabbath best, the synagogue's officials tried to be just as elegant—and modern. They valiantly attempted to retain their dignity while punishing members of the congregation who had lost theirs. "Because you, Mr. Schwartz [or Cohen or Goldman] have created a disturbance in the *shul* during the period of the prayers, maligned the officers and used base language, you are hereby fined one dollar," the minutes dutifully record—and record again.

In addition to a galaxy of synagogues large and small, the ghetto also contained a number of institutions designed to serve the community's varied religious needs. "First-class" kosher butcher shops and restaurants where the dietary laws were strictly observed as well as outlets where mat-zoh (the unleavened bread consumed during the Passover holiday) was made by manufacturers like Finesilver's Matzoh Baking Company—"We sell the most kosher matzoh of the highest quality for the lowest price"— were within a stone's throw of one another. Moreover, virtually every block or so contained a talmud torah, an afternoon Hebrew school where boys between the ages of 5 and 13 learned the ABCs of Judaism. (Girls were taught at home, by their mothers.) Many a young scholar tended to regard the hours devoted to studying Torah, the five books of Moses, as a theft of time better spent playing stickball or hanging out at the local candy store. On the other hand, he probably relished the annual "Passover bonfire," the traditional outdoor ritual of burning wheat products on the eve of the festival of Passover. (During the week of Passover, which com-memorates the exodus of the Jews from Egypt, where they were enslaved, to the Promised Land of Canaan, where they were set free, the eating of

Rubenstein & Glickman, a Chicago delicatessen, catered to the culinary needs of local Jewish residents.

CARNEGIE HALL
Thursday Afternoon, Nov. 30, 1905
At 2.30 o'clock

Exercises

IN

Celebration of the Two Hundred and Fiftieth Anniversary of the Settlement of the Jews in the United States 1655=1905

PROGRAMME

The musical programme is in charge of Dr. Frank Damrosch, assisted by members of the People's Choral Union, who have most courteously volunteered their services, and by the New York Symphony Orchestra. Mr. Frank L. Sealy at the Organ.

1. OVERTURE . . . *Mendelssohn*
   "March of the Priests from "Athalie"

2. PRAYER . . . .
   REVEREND JOSEPH SILVERMAN, D.D.
   Rabbi Temple Emanu-El, New York City

3. CHORUS . . . *Mendelssohn*
   From Oratorio "Elijah"
   "He, watching over Israel, slumbers not, nor sleeps. Shouldst thou, walking in grief, languish, He will quicken thee."

4. INTRODUCTION . . . .
   JACOB H. SCHIFF, Esq.
   Chairman of the Executive Committee

5. ADDRESS
   Honorable GROVER CLEVELAND

6. KOL NIDRE . . . . *Bruch*
   Solo Violoncello, MR. LEO SCHULZ

Programme continued on second page following

The anniversary of the first Jewish settlement in America was celebrated in New York with prayers, speeches, and music and attended by high-ranking politicians as well as religious leaders.

bread and other foods containing wheat is forbidden by Jewish law.) The "Passover bonfire," wrote a reporter for the *New York Sun,* is "as big and as enthusiastic a celebration [for the Jewish boy] as the 4th of July is for the American small boy of other faiths."

Not every ghetto boy and girl or their parents strictly observed Passover, learned proper Hebrew, or attended religious services, even on the High Holidays, the holiest days in the Jewish calendar. Many were downright hostile, preferring to put their faith in socialism rather than in God; some were simply indifferent. Others sought consolation elsewhere. In America's great ghettoes, explained social worker Charles Bernheimer in his classic 1905 account of the Jewish immigrant experience, *The Russian Jew in the United States,* philosophers, skeptics, and atheists abound. For them, as well as for those determined to keep the faith, America held out much promise.

Certainly everyone who gathered at Carnegie Hall in New York City on Thanksgiving Day, November 30, 1905, to mark the end of the 250th anniversary of Jewish settlement in America seemed to think so. After all, they had history on their side. "America has been the brightest spot in the history of the Jews," trilled the *American Hebrew,* one of the community's leading Jewish newspapers and an active participant in the festivities, not just a recorder of the event. That thousands of eastern European Jews sought refuge in the United States each year was nothing new, the paper pointed out. This most recent migration, it noted, was part of a much larger pattern, one that stretched as far back as 1654, when 23 refugees from Recife, Brazil—

many of them children—first sought the safety of America's shores. Ever since then, the United States "has been a haven of rest, of freedom from persecution and tyranny," a place that "chases [away] the wrinkles of gloom" from the souls of the Jewish people.

Drawing on the same kind of extravagant language fancied by the *American Hebrew,* speaker after speaker at the anniversary celebration, from former U.S. President Grover Cleveland to Jacob H. Schiff, American Jewry's leading philanthropist, sang America's praises. Their remarks generated great bursts of applause "from the floor to the roof" of the great concert hall, reported *The New York Times,* which featured the story on its front page. The paper also pointed out that the hall was "lavishly and artistically decorated" for the occasion with red, green, and gold bunting and lots of American flags. When the speech-makers finally retired from the stage, 50 members of the Downtown Cantors Association, a group made up of the religious specialists who lead Jewish worshipers in prayer, took their place. Joined by a mighty chorus under the baton of Frank Damrosch, a well-known New York City conductor, they performed a medley of Jewish and American songs. This, too, was rapturously received by the enthusiastic crowd. The cantors and chorus sang so well, in fact, that the press widely praised their performance, saying it would have done credit to the Metropolitan Opera. Even Macy's, one of the country's leading department stores, got in the spirit of things by offering specially priced copies of *The Jew in America,* the "souvenir volume" of the 250th anniversary. This celebration, declared the department store, is "one of the most important events in the history of American Judaism." But then, Joseph Silverman, rabbi of Temple Emanu-El, a synagogue renowned throughout the nation for the beauty of its architecture and the eminence of its membership, put it best. "The American people are our people and we are an American people," he said in a special Sabbath sermon devoted to the relationship between America and its Jewish citizens. "We have practiced the lessons of assimilation and in thought,

Banker Jacob H. Schiff, who made his fortune at Kuhn, Loeb and Company, a family firm, contributed generously to many Jewish causes. These included relief for Jewish victims of the Russian czar and funds to establish the Jewish Division in the New York Public Library. He also financed a new translation of the Bible into English.

sentiment, patriotism and devotion to our political institutions we are one with the American people." Amen to that, said the members of Silverman's congregation, proud Jews and proud Americans.

The congregants of Emanu-El were also Reform Jews, members of a movement that had started in Germany in the early 19th century to modernize Judaism. Where traditional Jews placed a premium on the traditions of the past and were reluctant to alter them in any way, Reform Jews saw things differently: Looking to the future, they did away with many of the practices that had for centuries rendered the Jews a people apart. Reform Judaism, explained Rabbi Kaufmann Kohler, one of its leading lights, has "reconciled modern life with religion." It has, he said, replaced the dead language of Hebrew by the living one of English and discarded antiquated customs of the past like the dietary laws and the wearing of *yarmulkes* (head-coverings) while at prayer. Reform Judaism, Kohler told his followers, "is a system of religious and ethical truths; ceremonies being only the means to higher ends, not ends in themselves."

Years earlier, in 1824, a number of young Charleston, South Carolina, Jews, headed by a journalist named Isaac Harby, tried to put into practice what Kohler would later preach. Claiming that Sabbath services were much too long, too boring, and far too noisy, they petitioned the synagogue's powers-that-be to institute a number of changes. (A visitor to Charleston's synagogue confirmed these charges. Disapprovingly, he noted that only a "very slight check seems to be imposed upon the usual inclinations of the children," meaning they ran around and made a lot of noise.) Make the services shorter, suggested the petitioners; use less Hebrew; and introduce an "English discourse" or sermon so that the congregation "should know something of [their] religion."

But the petition was rejected. Angered and disheartened, the group took the unprecedented step of seceding from the synagogue and forming its own, which they grandly called the Reformed Society of Israelites. With high hopes, they set about instituting nothing less than a "Jewish reformation" in the United States and for nearly 10 years worked hard at it—but to no avail. Ahead of its time, the new society was unable to generate enough financial or moral support to sustain itself and, by the early 1830s, it was no more.

In the years that followed, "Jewish reformation" received a new lease on life. The cause began to attract a growing number of followers, many of them German Jews who, in the 1830s and 1840s, emigrated to America along with thousands of their countrymen in search of economic and personal freedom. Swelling the Jewish population to about 150,000 on the eve of the Civil War, this generation of Jewish immigrants fanned out across the country. "From the newly gotten Santa Fe to the confines of New Brunswick and from the Atlantic to the shores of the western sea, synagogues are springing up as if by magic," lyrically wrote one American Jew at the time, imbuing the powerful national ideal of manifest destiny—the notion that Americans were destined to conquer the entire continent—with a Jewish aura. Some Jewish settlers had already belonged to a Reform synagogue back home or knew someone who did. Others became Reform Jews only after they had lived a while in Santa Fe or New Brunswick. In any event, once this new form of Judaism was clearly and eloquently "explained" to them, the "Jewish masses," confidently predicted Rabbi Isaac Mayer Wise, would be entirely "susceptible to Reform."

Under the leadership of charismatic, visionary leaders like Wise, Reform Judaism did grow stronger. Born in Bohemia, the son of a poor Jewish schoolteacher, young Isaac seemed destined to follow in his father's footsteps, teaching small children and preaching from time to time in the local synagogue. Faced with such bleak prospects, he became restless. "I had grown heartily weary of Europe," Wise wrote in his diary before deciding to emigrate. In 1846, at the age of 27, the schoolteacher packed his bags and made his way, together with his wife and child, "much luggage and little money," to the "strange land" of America. For eight long, controversial years he lived in Albany, New York, where, as rabbi of one congregation after another (and Albany was then a small town), he stirred up lots of trouble with his radical ideas. "The reforming spirit was innate in me; it was my foremost characteristic," Wise gamely acknowledged, adding that his lot in life was to "reform and improve the

The majestic interior of Cincinnati's Plum Street Temple, founded by Isaac Mayer Wise and designed in ornate, Moorish style, was evidence of the success of Reform Judaism in America. The building was placed on the National Register of Historic Places in 1972.

world." But not, apparently, in Albany, for in 1854 the rabbi moved to Cincinnati, the Queen City of the West, where he would live out his days. Careful to avoid the kind of controversy that had roiled his first decade in America, Wise slowly established a Reform presence in that fast-growing city. Eventually, he not only succeeded in transforming Cincinnati into the capital of Reform Judaism, home to Hebrew Union College, where Reform rabbis received their training, and the Union of American Hebrew Congregations of America, the voice of Reform Jewry at the grass roots. Wise also succeeded in bringing order and coherence to the movement as a whole. "There is life and energy in this new Judaism," he liked to say, underscoring its break with the past.

Throughout his long life (Wise died in 1900, at the age of 81), the grand old man of Reform Judaism was sure of himself and of his effect on people. Once, in Charleston, where he had been invited to deliver a series of lectures, Wise attended a "grand dinner" at the home of a local Jewish notable. Later that night, he wrote in his diary: "I was surrounded by a circle of ladies in the drawing-room who employed all manner of feminine wiles to attract my attention. It was [as] though we were in paradise." Women, however, were not the only ones who found him attractive. The "hold" which Dr. Wise has upon all "the people is astounding. . . . They cling to [him]," wrote the traditionally minded Joseph Abraham in 1859, noting with dismay that their hometown of Cincinnati was "so filled with reform doctrines, that it requires a strong body and mind not to inhale these pernicious vapors."

Most American Jews, however, did not share Mr. Abraham's negative opinion of Reform Judaism (or of Rabbi Wise). In the years after the Civil War, they embraced it wholeheartedly. Where synagogues were traditionally modest, humble structures in which men and women sat apart,

Like many other Reform temples, Temple Emanuel in Helena, Montana, was built in Moorish style. Even in the far West, such substantial structures testified to the economic and religious resilience of Jewish immigrants.

Reform Jews in San Francisco, Cincinnati, Chicago, Atlanta, and New York built grand houses of worship, which they called temples rather than synagogues. These were typically complete with organs, choir lofts, and beautifully finished wooden pews in which men and women sat side by side.

Inspiring thousands, the tenets of Reform Judaism spread from coast to coast. "Everywhere the temples of Israel, the monuments of progressive Judaism, as though touched by a magic wand, rise in proud magnificence and proclaim with a thundering voice, we are right and you are wrong," thundered Isaac Mayer Wise, certain about Reform Judaism's glorious future. Rabbi Adolf Moses of Mobile, Alabama, shared his teacher's vision—and then some. "From America, salvation will go forth," he predicted. "In this land, Judaism—Reform Judaism—will celebrate its greatest triumph."

Blessed with leaders who could turn a phrase, American Jews were also blessed with abundant optimism. Whether members of a Reform temple or an orthodox *shul*, they felt sure they could "deal effectively and happily with the great task of Americanization" while remaining committed Jews. Their children, though, were another matter entirely. "Our American-born youth have seen neither the Russian, Rumanian, Galician, Austrian, Hungarian, or German life," observed Rabbi Herbert Goldstein, the rabbi of a New York synagogue. "They have only seen American life." With no exposure to the traditions of the past, American Jewish boys and girls might have little feel for things Jewish, he worried. They might even slip away.

To make sure this did not happen in the years preceding World War I, the American Jewish community sought to appeal to its children on their own terms. Sponsoring father-son basketball games and mother-daughter teas, it published brightly illustrated, breezy magazines like *Helpful Thoughts* to "interest the normal American boy or girl" in Jewish matters. This monthly magazine was filled with uplifting articles on the "boyhood" of Moses, the biblical Jewish leader, and the "girlhood" of Queen Esther, the Persian Jewish heroine. It dispensed information and advice as well. A column titled "Jewish Customs and Ceremonies," for example,

introduced young readers to the "charms and delights" of Jewish holiday traditions like Hanukkah ("Our children of today do not know what they miss."). Another column penned by a "loving grandmother" encouraged American Jewish boys and girls to keep the Sabbath, to celebrate all of the Jewish festivals, and to recite the *sh'ma,* a traditional Jewish prayer, at bedtime. "Before going off to sleep, why not try an experiment and say good night to God. . . . Try this for a few nights and then write to me— tell me whether the night still seems so dark."

Meanwhile, Jewish boys and girls approaching adolescence spent several afternoons a week in preparation for their bar mitzvah or confirmation, two events that loomed large on the American Jewish calendar. Dating back to the 13th century, the bar mitzvah service marked the moment when, at age 13, the Jewish boy assumed full responsibility for his actions. Confirmation was a much newer ritual: Invented in the 19th century by Reform Jews in Germany, it marked the religious coming of age of girls as

In the United States, age-old Jewish holidays such as Purim received a new lease on life when transformed into a masquerade party for children.

The December Dilemma

Over the years, the nation's increasingly exuberant embrace of Christmas has made many American Jews uncomfortable. A religious tradition not their own, Christmas sets them apart. Today, Jews in the United States have all sorts of strategies for addressing their feelings of isolation, from workshops to online chat rooms. At the beginning of the 20th century, though, they made use of the popular press to clear the air, as in this 1906 article "How a Jew Regards Christmas" in The Ladies' Home Journal *magazine:*

As developed in recent decades, and most especially in the United States, Christmas has come to be the symbol and expression of the tenderest sympathies to which the heart of man may throb in responsive rhythm. No longer speaking the harsh dialect of dogmatic scholasticism, it phrases its wider message in the flowing vocabulary of the all-including humanities. . . . Its song of brotherhood outruns the halting metres of sect and sept, of clan and class. Sweeping with the stars the flight through the zones, its proclamation of good will awakens answering echoes under every sky.

What about the Jew? Does he have part in the unifying joy of the rare hour when differences of station and origin are fused in the consciousness of equivalence and equality of all men? . . .

In this country, as in England, the Jew rejoices that the Christmas sentiment is speedily and beautifully progressing toward realization in action. And when he sees the lights leap into glory in his neighbors' homes he breathes forth a fervent prayer for their happiness. As far as in him lies he helps make their joy more genuine. He gladly contributes his part to the happiness of his friends, and such as share with him the hospitality of his domestic hearth, but are not of his religious fraternity.

For himself and his own, however, as yet he prefers to wait. He kindles his less radiant Hanukah lamps, and in their more modest glow reads the prophecy of a more inclusive advent when Peace will prevail on God's earth, War will be forgotten, Prejudice will be unknown, and love of Man for Man will be the Worship uniting in one fellowship all of God's children.

The lighting of candles at a bar mitzvah ceremony, which celebrates a 13-year-old boy's coming of age, has become one of American Jewry's traditional practices.

well as boys and was usually held upon their 15th or 16th birthday. The bat mitzvah, a 20th-century invention, marked a girl's coming of age, either at 12 or 13.

European Jews did not make too much of either the bar mitzvah or confirmation. Though they were recognized as important events, they were typically celebrated modestly, with little fanfare. In the Old World, the bar mitzvah boy would be called to read the Torah for the first time. Then, after reciting a number of traditional prayers in Hebrew, he would deliver a little speech, usually in Yiddish, the day-to-day language of eastern European Jews, and that was that. In contrast, confirmation resembled a high-school graduation. Small groups of girls and boys would demonstrate their mastery of the rudiments of Judaism by delivering a series of speeches, usually in German, on the meaning of Jewish life. A small community reception would follow.

American Jews, however, made much ado over the bar mitzvah boy, showering him with gifts and praising him to the skies. "Our Jewish brethren," noted Rabbi Moses Weinberger as early as 1887, had completely transformed a simple event into the "greatest of holidays. . . . Every

The confirmation class of Temple Beth Israel in Houston, Texas, in 1910. Confirmation was a sort of ceremony held by Reform Jews to celebrate graduation from religious school.

year, boys by the hundreds celebrate their *bnei mitzvah* [plural of bar mitzvah] amid enormous splendor and great show." Confirmation, too, was accompanied by much excitement: The celebrants practiced their speeches until they (and every member of their family) knew the entire thing by heart while their parents anxiously consulted with the caterer over the private reception they would host later that day and relatives shopped for an appropriate gift.

While the people fussed, their rabbis fretted, anxious lest the bar mitzvah boy or confirmant lose sight of the fact that this was a profoundly religious occasion, not an exercise in "loot gathering" or merrymaking. The rabbis, of course, had every reason to be concerned about excessive frivolity. But then Jewish parents, who were becoming increasingly at home in America, had every reason to celebrate their good fortune and that of their children. Putting the past behind them, they welcomed the future. No wonder, then, that American Jews of all ages and religious backgrounds glorified the bar mitzvah and confirmation. As much a collective rite of passage as a personal, individual one, these two popular events symbolized American Jewry's coming of age as well.

In the years that followed World War I, American Jewry not only came of age but matured rapidly. It had little choice in the matter. The outbreak of World War I, which ravished European Jewry, had temporarily put an end to immigration from abroad while the passage, in 1921 and again in 1924, of restrictive U.S. legislation permanently closed America's doors to new immigration. No longer able to depend on the Old World, American Jews learned to draw on their own resources. By the time World War II erupted, a decade and a half later, an increasing proportion of the American Jewish population had been born on native, rather than foreign, soil and felt thoroughly at home in America. There are no "ifs, ands or buts" about it, Rabbi Morris Kertzer, a Jewish army chaplain, told an interviewer from *Look* magazine. American Jews consider themselves Americans through and through.

Other Americans, however, doubted the Jews' patriotism and loyalty. When it came time during the late 1930s and early 1940s to open the country's doors to European Jewish refugees fleeing Hitler's deadly policies, they slammed them shut. Only those lucky enough to have a relative or a business associate in the United States who was willing to support them and would sign a legal document to that effect were able to enter. This slender piece of paper on which so many hopes rested was called an affidavit. Peter Frohlich's family, which hailed from Berlin, was among the lucky ones. "The affidavit! How often did I hear that magical word spoken with longing or with satisfaction during those months, as German Jews frantic to get out did what my father was doing: searching American telephone books for long-lost relatives or only for someone with a name that resembled their own." In 1939, the Frohlichs left their beloved homeland for Cuba, where they remained until they were finally allowed into the United States in 1941.

In 1940, seven years after arriving in the United States from Germany, physicist Albert Einstein became a naturalized American citizen. His wife, Margot, is at right.

The Frohlichs were joined in their pursuit of safety and freedom by thousands of German Jewish and other refugees from Nazi Germany. Some, like composer Arnold Schoenberg and physicist Albert Einstein, were world-renowned personalities; most, however, were not. Ordinary people, lawyers and doctors, shopkeepers and housewives, they had been respectable and hardworking, loyal and proud German citizens until Hitler and his minions transformed them into outcasts. Some of these refugees went to Hollywood where, as directors, cinematographers, and composers, they had a profound impact on America's film industry; others like the Frohlich family went to places like Denver, where one of the first things they did was to change their names. Peter and his family followed the lead of a cousin who had changed his first name, Hanns, to Jack, and his last name, Frohlich, to Gay. "Americans found Frohlich hard to spell and impossible to pronounce," Peter explained. Besides, "Hanns—or, rather Jack—wanted to say farewell, as categorically as he could, to the country of his birth in behalf of the country of his future. We applauded and imitated his decision: my father, Moritz, became Morris; I translated my middle name, Joachim, to Jack, and all three of us adopted my cousin's choice for a family name. I became Peter Gay."

While the Schoenbergs went to Los Angeles and the Gays to Denver, the Kirchheimers began their new lives in Washington Heights, a neighborhood in the northernmost part of Manhattan. There, amid its modest brick apartment houses, hilly streets, and breathtaking views of the Hudson River (to some it resembled the familiar Rhine), they, together with some 20,000 of their German Jewish coreligionists, many of them from the city of Frankfurt, started all over. Preserving their links with a culture from which they had been violently uprooted, the German Jewish residents of Washington Heights, an enclave they themselves dubbed *das vierte reich*, or the Fourth Reich (a wry reference to Hitler's Third Reich), continued to speak and read German, to dine on German food and to practice their religion much as they had back home, in the company of their own kind.

Some, like the members of K'hal Adas Jeshurun, a leading Frankfurt Jewish congregation, successfully reestablished themselves in the New World, replicating the network of religious schools, charitable organizations, and kosher food stores that had long characterized this vibrant community. Others, like Alice Oppenheimer, a 1938 emigré from Mannheim, started afresh. Together with her husband, she organized a brand-new synagogue where Jews from Germany might feel at home, regardless of the city or village from which they came. "We didn't have anything against the American congregation but we only wanted to be a little bit more together," she recalled of her initial efforts at renting space downstairs from an established, and proudly American, synagogue. "We thought that maybe all hardship gets easier if you carry it together." Oppenheimer's neighbors in Washington Heights apparently felt the same way: Within a few years they had formed 29 different synagogues in Washington Heights, a testament to the human need for fellowship and solidarity.

In the wake of World War II and the complete destruction of European Jewry by Nazi Germany and its allies, American Jewry's sense of itself grew stronger still. Earlier, America had refused to admit Europe's increasingly harassed and dispossessed Jews into the U.S. After the war,

Both the newly-arrived and the long-established members of one Los Angeles family celebrate a Passover seder, or ritual meal.

to come to America when, in the 1970s and again during the 1990s, they were permitted to emigrate from the former Soviet Union. The arrival of 300,000 urban, educated Jews from the former Soviet Union during those 20 years, the latest in a long line of Jewish immigrants, completed a cycle of history that had begun a century earlier with the first large-scale Russian Jewish migration to the United States. Like their ancestors, Soviet Jews, fleeing political repression and persecution, came as families. Settling in Los Angeles, Chicago, New York, and Boston, they fashioned a distinctive approach to their Jewish identity or, as one Soviet Jewish immigrant of the 1980s put it, "We are Jewish in our way."

With strong ties to but little formal knowledge of Judaism (in the former Soviet Union, Jewish life, from attendance at synagogue to the study of Hebrew and Jewish texts, was banned and forced underground), Soviet Jews like Maxim expressed their Jewishness largely in ethnic terms. They continued to do so in America as well. Bar and bat mitzvah celebrations, for instance, an increasingly popular practice among the new immigrants, were routinely held in a Russian restaurant, where most of the celebrants felt at home, rather than a synagogue, where they did not. ("Have your birthday, anniversary, wedding, bar mitzvah here with us," advertised one Russian restaurant in the heart of Brighton Beach, New York, where many Soviet Jews came to live during the 1970s and 1980s.) Following one such celebration that blended elements of Jewish tradition, including the traditional Hebrew blessing over the Torah, with American birthday rituals like the singing of "Happy Birthday" and numerous vodka toasts, one guest, a recent immigrant, was moved to tears by the proceedings. "This was the first, the very first, bar mitzvah I've ever been to," she explained. "It was really nice to see, especially for us who, you know, in the Soviet Union, were Jewish but hid it. . . . [This] was great!"

Freeing Soviet Jews to lead fuller lives, America also enabled them to delight in their new-found Jewish identity. In this instance, as in so many others that characterized the Jewish experience in the New World, Jewish immigrants from the former Soviet Union joined others from Bialystok and Budapest, Vilna, Frankfurt, and Recife, Brazil, in finding America to be the answer to their prayers.

Chapter 4

In the Land of the Flowery Flag: Immigrants of the Late 20th Century

The Sri Venkateshwara Temple in Atlanta was built according to traditional temple design. Like other Hindu temples in Malibu, Hawaii, and across America, it is noted for its ornate sculptured plastering.

U p in the southern California hills, just north of Malibu, stands the majestic Sri Venkateshwara Temple, the largest Hindu shrine in the Western Hemisphere. Built in 1981 by expert craftsmen and temple builders brought from India, the shrine, said the *Los Angeles Times,* is a "sight to behold." With its nine domed towers encasing carved statues of the Hindu gods, gold-topped cupolas, and intricate carvings of lions and dragons, elephants and lotus blossoms, the temple looks like something straight out of Hollywood. But it is real, a place where thousands of Hindus go to pray and congregate, a place where East meets West.

Miles away, in the San Gabriel Valley, stands another dazzling sight, the Fo Kuang Shan Hsi Lai Temple, a Buddhist religious complex with pagoda-shaped roofs, rice paddies, and guardian lions that replicate the Fo Kuang Shan Temple in Taiwan. Sikh *gurdwaras* (temples) in Phoenix, Arizona; a Taoist temple in Denver, Colorado; a Jain center in Blairstown, New Jersey, as well as more than a thousand mosques from whose slender minarets Muslim worshipers from coast to coast are called to prayer, complete the portrait: This is what religion looks like in late 20th-century America. As *Time* magazine observed in 1993, "The world has never seen a nation as religiously diverse as the United States."

Since the 1970s, the arrival of several million immigrants from the Far East, the Middle East, and Southeast Asia has enriched the religious fabric of American life in ways unimaginable only a few decades earlier. They come from China, Japan, Korea, and the Philippines; from Thailand, Laos, Cambodia, Vietnam, India, Pakistan, Iran, Egypt, and Lebanon, bringing forms of religious architecture, styles of prayer, and religious beliefs once foreign to the United States. Many newcomers, directing their prayers to Allah or Buddha rather than Christ, sit on the floor, on prayer mats and rugs, rather than in pews, and chant *sutras* rather than sing hymns. Others, coming from countries like Korea with a strong Christian presence, add to the already variegated nature of American Christianity by giving rise to hundreds of churches where services are conducted entirely in Korean. In each instance, these new immigrants have extended the range and meaning of religion in the United States.

America's latest wave of immigrants constitutes a highly diverse group whose members differ from one another in terms of their faith, class, and level of education as well as country of origin. They also vary from one another in their reasons for emigrating. Some have come seeking political asylum, others a better way of life; some as refugees, others as students. Some were driven out; others came of their own accord. And yet, despite their diversity, America's newest immigrants hold several things in common. For one, they owe their presence in the United States to a liberalization of the nation's immigration policies. In 1965, after more than a century of exclusionary practices, the government agreed to permit 20,000 immigrants a year from each Asian and Middle Eastern country to enter the United States. Seizing the new opportunity to emigrate, half of all recent arrivals these days hail from the East.

For another thing, the "new immigrants," like those before them, are bound together by their belief in the promise of America, or as *The New York Times* reported in 1986, for them the "United States is still the land of hope." Take Khounphom Sone, for instance. A refugee from Laos, Sone, together with his wife, a former noodle-shop waitress, and their five children fled their war-torn country, a casualty of the Vietnam War, with the idea of coming to the United States. "I want to go to Brooklyn very much," he told *The Times*. "Because there is my brother." In some cases, the post-1965 wave of immigrants included people like Sone and his brother, who were the first in their family to live in the United States. Other cases included those whose collective history in this country, like that of the Japanese, the Koreans, and the Sikhs, goes back at least a hundred years, to the turn of the century and, in the case of the Chinese, long before that.

Several thousand Chinese, all men, arrived in this country during the California gold rush of the 1840s and 1850s, intending to work for a few years, save some money, and return home to their families. "Quite a large number of Celestials have arrived among us of late, enticed thither by the golden romance that has filled the world," observed the *Daily Alta California* in 1852, referring to the Chinese. Working either as independent prospectors or as miners, Chinese immigrants grew steadily in number: in 1851 there were 2,716; the following year there were more than 20,000. As profits declined, Chinese laborers left the gold mines for the railroads, helping to build the Central Pacific Railroad, among others. The rugged mountains of California, noted one eyewitness, "swarm with Celestials, shoveling, wheeling, carting, drilling and blasting rocks and earth." Once

California's gold fever of the 1850s was felt as far away as China. Many Chinese emigrants, called "Gum Shan Hok," or "Guests of Gold Mountain," took the gamble and became gold miners, as shown in this 1868 photograph by Eadweard Muybridge.

work on the great transcontinental railroads was completed, the Chinese found jobs as factory workers and farmhands, only to discover that white workers increasingly resented their presence. Pushed out of the mainstream economy, the Chinese had no choice but to create their own ethnic economy fueled by stores, restaurants, and laundries. Still they continued to arrive. All told, more than 300,000 Chinese emigrated to the United States between 1851 and 1882, when Congress passed the Chinese Exclusion Act barring "Chinese laborers" from entering the country.

During those years, nearly half of all Chinese returned home, as planned; most, however, remained in the United States. Relatively small in number, especially when compared with their European counterparts, and hemmed in by considerable racial and economic prejudice, the Chinese kept to themselves. Derided as a "current of barbarians" whose Buddhist, Taoist, or Confucian religion had "nothing spiritual" about it, or so insisted Senator John P. Jones of Nevada in 1876, they preferred to live among their own kind, in self-contained Chinatowns where, wrote one observer, "Chinese faces delight the vision and Chinese voices greet the ear." Most of those faces and voices belonged to men: Chinese women, either reluctant to leave or forbidden from leaving their ancestral homeland, were few and far between. It was not until 1907 that Chinese men, claiming the rights of American citizens, were able to bring over their wives. Between 1907 and 1920, 10,000 Chinese women joined their husbands in the New World, or what some called the land of the "flowery flag."

In the meantime, the "Celestials" lived out their lives in the company of other men, where they practiced the tenets of their faith quietly, either in the privacy of their own homes or in congregations whose exteriors were so modest and unassuming, so unchurchlike, as to give little

Although the Chinese in America preferred to wear traditional clothing, there were times when phrase books like this one came in handy.

ENGLISH - CHINESE PHRASEOLOGY.

汝有乜貨物出賣
What goods have you for sale?

樣樣都有
I have all kinds.

我想買条好褲
I want to get a pair of your best pants.

地爱乜價銀
What do you ask for them?

汝能减少吟
Can you take less for them?

不能先生
I can not, sir.

hint of what went on inside. No wonder the "customs of the Chinese" were so little known and frequently misunderstood, wrote folklorist Stewart Culin in 1890, hoping to improve the situation. Because "most observers have been content to record only those features which appeared to them strange and unusual," the overwhelming majority of Americans were left in the dark, he said, about the richness and complexity of Chinese life. Carefully describing the way the Chinese honored their dead (with candles and incense), celebrated the birth of a child (with gifts in red paper packages), and marked the new year (with special foods), Culin hoped to set the record straight. "The dinner is the principal feature of all holiday observances, and at such dinners every one eats to repletion," he wrote, noting how the "food itself, the table service, and methods of cooking, are always exclusively

Chinese." The way the Chinese worshiped their gods was just as unique. "Many laundries and shops contain small shrines . . . before which incense and candles are burned," he explained, adding that "large and expensive shrines . . . with implements for divination, are found in all their guild halls and lodge rooms." Though taken with the Chinese way of life, Culin could not help wondering about its future. In the "restless Western world," where change is constant, how long would it be, he asked, before these ancient customs faded away?

Like the Chinese, Japanese immigrants also worried about the future. Initially, things looked bright for the tens of thousands who, in the 1880s and 1890s, left Japan for Hawaii or the U.S. mainland, lured by the

The biggest day in the Chinese calendar is the New Year, or spring festival, which is celebrated in late January or February with a joyous, noisy parade. The Chinese transported this ancient tradition to Chinatowns across America. This 1928 celebration in Los Angeles is typical.

Transmitting Tradition

When it comes to tradition, the American-born members of a family are often at a disadvantage. As this excerpt from Maxine Hong Kingston's celebrated 1975 novel The Woman Warrior: Memoirs of a Girlhood Among Ghosts *makes vividly clear, foreign-born parents do not always have the time, the inclination, or the tools to explain the meaning of age-old rituals. Meanwhile, their American-born children struggle to understand.*

Even the good things are unspeakable, so how could I ask about deformities? From the configurations of food my mother set out, we kids had to infer the holidays. She did not whip us up with holiday anticipation or explain. You only remembered that perhaps a year ago you had eaten monk's food, or that there was meat, and it was a meat holiday; or you had eaten moon cakes or long noodles for long life (which is a pun). In front of the whole chicken with its slit throat toward the ceiling, she'd lay out just so many pairs of chopsticks alternating with wine cups, which were not for us because there were a different number from the number in our family, and they were set too close together for us to sit at. To sit at one of those place settings a being would have to be about two inches wide, a tall wisp of an invisibility. Mother would pour Seagram's 7 [Scotch whiskey] into the cups and, after a while, pour it back into the bottle. Never explaining. How can Chinese keep any traditions at all? They don't even make you pay attention, slipping in a ceremony and clearing the table before the children notice specialness. The adults get mad, evasive, and shut you up if you ask. You get no warning that you shouldn't wear a white ribbon in your hair until they hit you and give you the sideways glare for the rest of the day. . . . You figure out what you got hit for and don't do it again if you figured correctly. But I think that if you don't figure it out, it's all right. Then you can grow up bothered by 'neither ghosts nor deities.' 'Gods you avoid won't hurt you.' I don't see how they kept up a continuous culture for five thousand years. Maybe they didn't; maybe everyone makes it up as they go along. If we had to depend on being told, we'd have no religion, no babies, no menstruation (sex, of course, unspeakable), no death.

prospect of earning a substantial wage—a dollar a day—as laborers. When the Japanese government announced the availability in 1885, following on the heels of the Chinese Exclusion Act of 1882, of 600 jobs to fill the void created by the sudden drop in the number of Chinese workers, 28,000 Japanese applied. In the years that followed, the Japanese authorities, who encouraged the emigration of both their male and female citizens to avoid overpopulation, watched with approval as the number of emigrants soared: Between 1885 and 1924, 200,000 Japanese moved to Hawaii and 180,000 relocated to the mainland.

Most, if not all, of the Japanese immigrants—migrant laborers who cultivated sugarcane in Hawaii, picked and canned fruit in California, or worked in the lumber mills of the Pacific Northwest—had little intention at first of settling permanently in the United States. Rather, they hoped to save enough money to enable them to return home to Japan, where they might comfortably live out the rest of their lives. "I planned to work three years in the United States to save 500 yen and then go back to Japan because if I had 500 yen in Japan I could marry into a farmer's household, using it for my marriage portion [dowry]," recalled one immigrant.

The Young Men's Christian Association, or YMCA, was active in helping immigrants from Asia and other lands familiarize themselves with life in America. This photo from the 1920s shows Japanese Americans in Western clothes participating in a dramatic skit.

Ultimately, though, 40 percent of all Japanese immigrants stayed. Turning to vegetable and berry farming, at which they prospered ("fresh green rows of strawberries reaching as far as the eye could see" was how one Japanese farmer described his fields), they grew increasingly rooted in America. Many dreamed of becoming farmers. Or, as one Japanese farmer put it:

> Resolved to become
> The soil of the foreign land,
> I settle down.
> America—where
> My three sons grow lustily
> More than a wayside stop.

Others chose to settle down in urban areas, creating a Little Tokyo in both San Francisco and Los Angeles, where the familiar sights, sounds, and foods of Japan drew thousands of *issei,* the Japanese word for immigrant or first-generation American. Many—sometimes as much as 39 percent in a given year—were women. Some came along with their husbands; others were brought over a few years later. And still others, like Ai Miyasaki, were picture-brides. In Japanese society, where marriages were arranged, often over long distances, prospective brides and grooms would frequently exchange photographs before meeting each other for the first time. That tradition continued in the New World as well. "When I told my parents about my desire to go to a foreign land," recalled Ai Miyasaki, "the story spread throughout the town. From here and there requests for marriage came pouring in just like rain!" As a result of the picture-bride, or *shashin kekkon* (literally, "photo marriage") system, thousands of women like Ai Miyasaki made their way to the United States. Thanks to their substantial presence, Japanese farmers and urban residents alike tended to lead a far more stable, family-centered

Even in America, the Japanese followed the tradition of arranged marriages, often preceded by an exchange of photos. These tiny photographs, dating from 1915, identified Ai Hitaka as a "picture-bride" and Ichihei Hitaka as her husband and were used by the U.S. Department of Labor for identification.

existence than the residents of Chinatown, where children were rare. In contrast, the American-born offspring of Japanese parents, known as *nisei,* were so numerous that by 1940 they comprised nearly two thirds of all Japanese in America.

The Bangle Buddhist Saturday School helped to keep Buddhist traditions alive in the New World. Dressed in their national costumes, the children of the school pose for a picture in front of their temple in Long Beach, California.

Religion, like family, also made for stability. Buddhism, the ancestral faith of many Japanese, was a "good influence" on the workers, believed the plantation bosses, who encouraged the establishment of Buddhist temples in Hawaii and the importation of Buddhist priests. Buddhism flourished in the continental United States as well, especially the Jodo Shinshu denomination, a branch of Amida, or Pure Land, Buddhism practiced by a majority of Japanese Buddhists. As early as 1898, 30 young Japanese residents of San Francisco organized the Young Men's Buddhist Association, the *Bukkyo Seinen Kai,* where they gathered on a weekly basis to study religious texts and socialize.

A year later, they sent a letter to Buddhist headquarters in Japan requesting that a Buddhist priest be assigned to San Francisco. Signed by 83 people, it read: "In eight directions are non-Buddhist forces surrounding the Japanese Buddhists, and we cannot be at ease. It is as if we are sitting on the point of a pin; no matter how we move, we will be pricked.

Our burning desire to hear the Teachings of Buddha is about to explode from every pore in our body." The Buddhist authorities, moved by this heartfelt declaration, sent two missionaries to San Francisco where, in short order, they began to conduct services, deliver sermons, and preside over the celebration of such Buddhist festivals as *Obon*, the Festival of the Dead. The two missionaries, later joined by several additional recruits, also brought a keen organizational sensibility to the task of providing Buddhists in the New World with "spiritual comfort" by forming a women's auxiliary—a sisterhood called the Buddhist Women's Association—that sponsored picnics and outings and set up congregations in Oakland, Sacramento, Fresno, and Palo Alto.

The hub of the Japanese community, the Buddhist temple or church, as it called itself in deference to convention, was also a source of comfort, especially during the 1910s and 20s, a time when Japanese faced growing hostility and the hardening of prejudice against them. Denied the right to own land and to become naturalized U.S. citizens, as much as a heightened feeling that the Japanese were "undesirable" made them feel unwelcome. "We try hard to be American but Americans always say you always Japanese," a member of the community observed sadly. "Irish become American and all time talk about Ireland; Italians become Americans even if do all time like in Italy; but Japanese can never be anything but Jap."

Under such conditions, the number of Buddhist congregations on the West Coast grew dramatically, to 25 by the mid-1920s. Earlier, some Japanese "had been hesitant in calling themselves Buddhists, considering such an act impudent in a Christian country," wrote sociologist Kosei Ogura at the time. The increasing hostility of that Christian country, however, made them realize the importance of Buddhism in their lives, and "naturally they sought the centers of their communal activity in their Buddhist churches." Subsequent developments, from the cessation of immigration in 1924 to the forcible "evacuation," as it was euphemistically called, of all Japanese, including those born in this country, to internment camps during World War II, reinforced the community's sense of vulnerability. "If I were alone," a Japanese resident of White River Valley, Washington, bitterly declared, "I might choose to return to Japan, but

now I have these children for whose sake I will stick it out to the bitter end." Though it would take years before the Japanese community felt at home in America, Buddhism, with its comforting belief in a better after-life, doubtless helped many of its members, like the long-time inhabitants of White River Valley, to "stick it out."

Korean immigrants, considerably fewer in number than either the Japanese or the Chinese, began to come to the United States—first to Hawaii, and then the mainland—following the Japanese invasion in 1903 and subsequent takeover of their country seven years later. Life under the Japanese was extremely harsh, recalled Whang Sa Sun, a high-school teacher. "Korea was like a jail and I was a prisoner." Under the Japanese, added another Korean immigrant to the United States, "No freedom. Not even free talking." The climate of political repression, coupled with the difficulty of making a living, prompted many Koreans like Whang Sa Sun

A 1993 gathering in Los Angeles marking Buddha's birthday. The shape of the wheel seen here is a symbol of unity and each of the eight spokes represents a different Buddhist tradition.

Identified only as Mr. A Lee, this Korean farm laborer was photographed in June 1912 in a Los Angeles work camp set up to accommodate seasonal workers. The farms and orchards of sunny California provided many jobs for those willing to do manual labor.

to consider leaving for Hawaii where, they were told by representatives from the sugarcane plantations, "gold dollars blossom on every bush," and "clothing grows on trees, free to be picked." Inspired by such images as well as by the prospect of earning $16 a month, a substantial sum by Korean standards, 6,700 Koreans, most of them young, single men, emigrated between 1903 and 1905. Women were not entirely absent from these ranks, though: Several hundred are believed to have accompanied their husbands to Hawaii or to have been mail-order or "picture" brides. I had heard a great deal about Hawaii, related one former picture-bride. "I wanted to come, so I sent my picture. Ah, marriage! Then I could get to America!"

For most Koreans, though, the promise of America was extremely short-lived. In 1905, the Japanese prohibited everyone, with the exception of wives and picture-brides, from leaving Korea. They hoped both to lessen the possibility of competition with Japanese laborers in the United States and to dampen a growing enthusiasm for a free-Korea movement among Koreans living abroad. At about the same time, a thousand or so Korean laborers and their families left Hawaii for the mainland. On the plantation, explained one worker, we were "treated no better than cows or horses." Some, hoping for a far better way of life, headed for Utah, where they worked in the copper mines, or went to Arizona, to work on the railroads. Most migrated to California, however, where they picked grapes in Sacramento, cultivated rice in Willows, or eked out a living as gardeners, janitors, and restaurant workers.

Too small in number to form a neighborhood, a Koreatown all their own, Korean immigrants made sure, though, to build a church. Thanks to the successful conversion efforts of Protestant missionaries, an estimated half of all Korean immigrants were already professing Christians by the time they reached Hawaii or the continental United States. In no time at all, they established their own houses of worship. A Korean Methodist Church could be found in San Francisco as early as 1905, followed a year later by a Korean Presbyterian Church in Los Angeles. At these and other congregations, where the Bible was read and prayers sung in their native language, Koreans proudly came together as a community. "A people without a country must have something to believe in and to hold on to," explained the pastor of one Korean congregation. "In Christian principles we have found a pattern for our future—both as individuals and as a nation." One of his parishioners, a female Korean immigrant, explained the church's appeal more simply and directly. "Sundays, I would dress up in my clean Sunday clothes and go to worship," she recalled. She felt "lots of enthusiasm and happiness in just being able to do something."

In the absence of a steady stream of new arrivals—the Japanese prohibition against emigration remained in force through World War II—the Korean community remained quite small. As late as 1920, it contained fewer than 2,000 souls, most of them men. Often taken for Chinese or Japanese by

The congregation of the Delano, California, Korean Methodist Church, flanked by American and Korean flags, proudly poses for a group picture in 1940.

111

Americans who had no idea that a country called Korea actually existed, the Koreans were long one of America's little-known, barely visible minorities. The Korean War of 1950–53 changed all that. For one thing, it put Korea on the map, literally and symbolically. For another, it virtually doubled the size of the Korean community in America, thanks to the arrival of 17,000 Koreans, the wives and adopted children of U.S. servicemen.

A decade later, the Korean community was no longer invisible. Between 1965 and 1985, as a result of America's new immigration policies, the Korean community began to grow by leaps and bounds, to the point where it numbered half a million people by the end of the eighties. Settling in New York and Los Angeles, among other places, that wave of Korean immigrants, many of them from educated, middle-class families, invigorated both cities by their presence. "What used to be Mexican-American, Japanese, and Jewish stores and businesses are now mostly Korean, with giant Oriental letters spread across their low-slung storefronts," wrote *Newsweek* in 1975, marveling at the change in Los Angeles, home to the largest concentration of Koreans outside of Korea. Other observers marveled at the stunning growth rate of the various Korean religious and cultural institutions, pointing out that as early as the mid-

1970s Los Angeles alone was home to 70 Korean churches, a dozen Buddhist temples, and more than 100 youth clubs. What accounted for this about-face? In America, Koreans have an opportunity to "breathe in its air of freedom," explained Kim Ta Tai. They have an opportunity to "change their destiny."

Where Koreans, then as now, came to settle and change their destiny, Asian Indians came in search of work. By the early years of the 20th century, more than 6,000 had emigrated to what one newspaper at the time called the "land of the Stars and Stripes," hoping to make more than the eight cents a day they typically made at home. All were men and all were commonly believed to be "Hindoo" (Hindus), which they were not. Most, in fact, were Sikhs; with some Hindus, and some Muslims. Arriving on the West Coast, they went to work on the railroads, where the Sikhs' distinctive white turbans, a sign of their religious commitment to wearing their hair unshorn, stood out against the ochre-colored landscape. "For miles their turbaned figures may be seen wielding crow-bar or shovel along the tracks," observed *Forum* magazine in 1910. Pushed out by hostile white workers who objected to working alongside the "Hindoo invaders," Indian immigrants later turned to agriculture where, as migrant farmhands, they filled a niche left vacant by the 1924 law excluding Chinese and Japanese laborers.

Through it all, Asian Indians retained their religious traditions. Even while living under the most punishing and harsh of conditions, they followed their religion's dietary laws (Muslims ate no pork; Hindus no meat), and observed the fast and feast days of their respective traditions. Sikh workers often even managed to erect a humble temple—"sometimes nothing but a shack," recalled one immigrant—where they might worship together. Later, with growing prosperity, the tiny Sikh community of Stockton, California, was able to build a far more elaborate, two-story house of worship known as a *gurdwara,* or "gateway of the guru" (a guru being a spiritual teacher) which, several times a year, drew Sikhs from all over California.

Still, it was hard to make a go of things. A community of lonely "uncles," Indian immigrants were far removed, both geographically and

A strong sense of community and pride in their roots characterizes Sikhs in America. The cropped beards and the colorful turbans wrapped around their heads distinguish Sikhs from members of other Hindu sects.

psychologically, from the families they had left behind. To make matters worse, discriminatory U.S. legislation cut them off from the rest of the country by forbidding them to own land or marry white women. Not surprisingly, many elected to return home. By 1940, the Asian-Indian community had dwindled to fewer than 2,500.

A generation later, however, everything had changed. Since 1965, more than 450,000 people from the Indian subcontinent have settled in the United States, transforming a moribund community into an extremely lively, diverse community of Hindus, Parsis, Sikhs, Jains, Buddhists, Christians, and Muslims. Different in every respect from the first wave of Asian-Indian immigrants, the second group emigrated as families, hailed largely from the middle class, and planned on settling permanently in the United States. "We came from India to get a better life here," explained Ratna Kumar, who, together with her husband and three children, emigrated from Hyderabad to Chicago in the early 1970s. The Shenoys, who met and married while both were graduate students in the United States, had a similar perspective. "We just felt that this country offered the best possible kind of freedom, both spiritual freedom, religious freedom, freedom to work, freedom to travel. And so we just felt that that's what we wanted to do," related Durga Shenoy, who became a citizen in 1974 after living in the United States for several years.

For some Asian-Indian families like the Shenoys, freedom took the form of cultivating a cultural rather than a religious form of Indian identity. Though both Mr. and Mrs. Shenoy were born and raised as Hindus, their children were not. In their Chicago household, Indian music and Indian food took the place of temple services and religious practice. "We did have a lot of Indian artifacts and things like that," noted their daughter, Padma. "But it wasn't overpowering in our house." A different atmosphere, though, prevailed in the homes of some of Padma's friends. "We'd go over to other people's homes, and they'd have a lot of Indian things in the house, or they'd have a little praying area, and the house would always smell of Indian food." The Nagars, a Brahman family from Gujarat, in northwestern India, were among the latter group of immigrants. The kitchen in their Midwestern suburban home contains a small countertop temple as well as a *tulsi* plant, which Hindus consider holy, while the family room is host to a large picture of Krishna. Sikh families

Central to Hindu temples is the altar. This drawing of one, in the Kadavul Temple in Hawaii, features a 6-foot-high 200-year-old bronze figure of the god Shiva, brought to the islands from southern India. On the step are offerings of food to the god.

in turn have made use of one of America's most popular institutions—the summer camp—to nurture a Sikh sensibility among their American-born children. Heirs to a tradition born 500 years ago in the Punjab region of northern India, young American Sikhs, it seemed, were often all too ignorant of its meaning and content. Our children can "chant rap songs but not Sikh scriptures, they can name the Ten Commandments but not the ten Sikh gurus," concerned parents told a reporter from *The New York Times* in June 1998.

Summer camp was one way to ameliorate the situation. At Logarh Retreat, a facility in Chambersburg, Pennsylvania, formerly known as Camp Robin Hood, a camper's day is filled with water sports and lessons in turban-tying (Sikh men traditionally do not cut their hair; they grow it long and cover it with a turban) and midnight discussions around the camp fire about Sikh culture—punctuated by lively performances of Gilbert and Sullivan, a long-standing tradition of summer camps everywhere. Camp has "really changed me," acknowledged Mandeep Singh Dhillon of Winchester, Virginia. "It turned me from this assimilated American guy into someone who's proud of [his] culture."

Like Sikhs and Hindus, Muslims were also proud of their ancient religious culture, which they brought with them to the New World. As early as the 1920s, a number of mosques and Islamic associations such as the Modern Age Arabian Islamic Society and the American Mohammedan Society could be found scattered across the United States. Wherever Arab peddlers plied their trade or Arab sailors gathered, from Ross, North Dakota, and Cedar Rapids, Iowa, in the west to Brooklyn, New York, in the east, they established a small Islamic community. It was not until the 1970s, though, that significant numbers of Muslims, many of them well-educated men and women, began to settle in the United States, at the rate of 25,000 to 35,000 a year. Some came from India and Pakistan; others from Albania and Yugoslavia; still others from the Middle East.

Feeling increasingly at home in America, members of the Muslim community have recently built more than 1,300 mosques and Islamic centers. Some are housed in modest storefronts. Others, like the Masjid Al Faatir Islamic Center in Chicago, can accommodate up to 3,000 worshipers at one time. Regardless of their size and scale, Islamic institutions hearten those of the Islamic faith. "The mosque plays a definite role here in keeping people within the faith," noted a Jordanian immigrant in 1983. "People are thinking about the religion more if a mosque is near. Even if they don't go, they still know the mosque is there; it helps." What also helped was a growing sense that, with several million members, Islam too was becoming an integral part of America. "When big shots get on a podium all over the United States, I would like the day to come when they all will say, 'Catholics, Protestants, Jews and Muslims,'" declared another Muslim immigrant. "I would love to see Islam included every single time that someone speaks about religion in America."

Latter-day immigrants from China and Japan no doubt feel the same way. After a long hiatus, they, like their ancestors before them, have returned to the United States. Between 1965 and 1984, as many as

419,373 Chinese settled in this country, together with 93,646 Japanese. Largely well-educated urban dwellers, they include men and women like Wing Ng, who left China in 1975 in search of greater cultural and economic opportunities. "The reason why I wanted to come to the United States is that I heard it is really freedom. That's the first thing. And the second was education." This new wave of immigrants, infusing the country's Chinatowns and other ethnic neighborhoods with renewed vitality, has given a new lease on life to age-old communities.

Finding strength in numbers—by 1990 the "new immigrant" population and its children exceeded 7 million people—its members seem far more secure about the viability of their respective religious traditions than their forebears did. These days, immigrants like M. Parthasarathy, manager of the Sree Venkateshwara Temple in southern California, feel

More and more mosques, like this one in Washington, D.C., define America's urban landscape. The series of arches is a typical architectural feature of a mosque, where Muslims come to pray and worship.

comfortable building religious structures—imposing ones at that—that proudly proclaim their Eastern origins. Several years ago, noted the leader of a suburban mosque, "a Muslim was afraid to identify himself as a Muslim. . . . But now, with so many Muslims coming and moving into the suburbs, more and more are making themselves known. I expect that in the near future, we will have twenty-five to thirty Islamic centers in this region." Many newcomers have also found religion looming larger in their lives than it had before. "I grew up in India, I consider myself a good Hindu, but I'd never had so many of these things until I came here," acknowledged one Indian immigrant, referring to the monthly meetings of the Organization of Hindu Malayalees, a congregation of Hindus from Kerala, in southern India, which features communal worship and the singing of devotional songs. Another who made a point of taking her children to temple on a regular basis put it this way: "I think Hinduism is more for personal internal religion than social religion and I think that what people are doing here is making [religion] more social than it is even in India." In the New World, she and other immigrants have noted, participation in religious activities becomes a way of affirming what was taken for granted in the Old: community.

Whether taking their children to temple or enrolling them in an after-school program where they might learn about Islam or Buddhism or Hinduism, immigrants from the Middle East and Southeast Asia invariably enlarged the scope of their religious institutions. "Back home," the temple or mosque was a house of worship. Here in America, like the church and the synagogue before it, the temple has become home to classes and play groups, weddings and funerals, political meetings and concerts as well as prayer services. As it came to assume a larger role in the lives of its devotees, the mosque was perceived as a center that ought to be a "nice place," related one Lebanese immigrant, a place to which parents could bring their children and "teach them their religion and their languages. Then once they get used to coming to the mosque, you will see them there regularly when they have the time." The nature of religious leadership changed too as priests and imams not only taught and led services, as they always had, but engaged in such new pursuits as counseling, politics, community relations, and even Boy Scout Jamborees. The imam, observed a congregant, is the "center" of the mosque, "so he is the one to be involved . . . with all these things."

Exposed to America and all of its material things, Asian immigrants in turn have radically transformed this nation. Its religious landscape, once shaped and defined by the great religious traditions of the West, by Christianity and Judaism, has had to make room for the great religious traditions of the East, whose belief systems, architecture, music, and way of life are a far cry from what most Americans have traditionally associated with religion. And as the landscape expanded to accommodate Hindus and Sikhs, Muslims and Buddhists, and their respective traditions, so too did the nation's religious vocabulary: Gurus and imams, mosques and temples are now as much a part of the language as rabbis, priests and pastors, churches and synagogues.

The destination of millions of "new immigrants," America since the 1960s might best be likened to a big tent. Anchored by two sturdy poles, one of religious pluralism and the other of religious freedom, that tent turns out to be roomy enough to include those who, years earlier, came from the West as well as those who, most recently, have come from the East.

Chapter 5

The Legacy of Immigration

O n a fine autumn day in 1893, some 4,000 people streamed into Chicago's Columbus Hall to celebrate the grand opening of the World's Parliament of Religions. As the Liberty Bell struck 10 times, each strike representing one of the world's great faiths, a "stately column" of religious leaders from around the globe filed into the hall. "Disciples of Christ, of Mohammed, of Buddha, Brahma and even Confucius," were all present, reported one keen-eyed observer, taking particular care to note the "strange robes, turbans and tunics, crosses and crescents, flowing hair and tonsured heads" among them. Jews, dressed in Western suits and ties, were also in attendance, as were Christian Scientists, Catholics, Theosophists, Ethical Culturists, African Methodist Episcopalians, and virtually "every grade" of Protestant. (Baptists, however, stayed away from the gathering, to protest the Sunday opening.)

His Eminence James Cardinal Gibbons, splendidly dressed in his red cardinal robes, opened the proceedings by offering a prayer. He no sooner intoned the words "Our Father who Art in Heaven" than a "rush of voices" met his own in a chorus of unity. "The supreme moment of the 19th century was reached," avidly recalled one participant. "Asia, Africa, Europe, America and the isles of the sea together called him Father. . . Jews, Mohammedans and all divisions of Christians seemed to be a rainbow of promise."

In an unprecedented event, representatives of the world's religions gathered in the heart of Chicago in 1893 in a show of religious tolerance. They hoped to set an example of peaceful coexistence to the rest of the world.

Likening itself to a "museum of faiths," the World's Parliament of Religions put the world's religions on display. Day after day for more than two weeks, thousands of visitors came both to see real-life Hindus, Buddhists, and Muslims and to hear them speak about their respective religious philosophies. Lectures on such topics as "What the Dead Religions Bequeath to the Living," "The Importance of a Serious Study of All Religions," and "The Impact of Religion on Married Life" punctuated the program. The sight of so many different religious personalities amicably sharing the stage with one another generated considerable excitement. Some participants heralded the event as the "beginning of a new epoch of brotherhood and peace." Others went further still. Moved by the ecumenical, cooperative spirit of the occasion, they pronounced it the "most important occurrence since the birth of Jesus."

In the end, little came of such predictions. After 17 days of goodwill, tolerance, and intellectual camaraderie, the delegates from China and India, the Middle East and the Midwest simply packed their bags and went home, as did those who had crowded Columbus Hall in eager anticipation of revelation and knowledge. In the years that followed, as the 19th century gave way to the 20th, no great demonstrations of brotherhood and peace ensued, either.

But all that is history. Today, with the 20th century given way to the 21st, we have an opportunity to reclaim the legacy of the World's Parliament of Religions—not by visiting a "museum of faiths," listening to a lecture, or attending a conference. All we have to do is take a good look at America or, better still, take a walk down the streets of any neighborhood on a Sunday morning. Note the number and variety of churches whose doors stand wide open to welcome worshipers: the Spanish Unity Ministerio de Cristianismo Práctico and the Korean Methodist New York Agape Church; St. Sebastian's and St. John the Divine, to name just a few. The local mosque, which marked its Sabbath on Friday, and the neighborhood synagogue, which celebrated it on Saturday, are also open and chock-a-block with activity, classes, lectures and meetings, social clubs and potluck suppers. Even rural America reflects the nation's religious diversity. In southeastern Iowa, in the small town of Columbus Junction (population: fewer than 2,000), the local Roman Catholic church, St. Joseph the Worker, celebrates two masses. The first is crowded with the descendants of northern European immigrants who founded the church more than a century ago; the second is filled to the rafters with the town's newest inhabitants: Mexican Americans.

As each new group of immigrants takes its place in the pews of a church built by its predecessors or builds its own, it not only adds something novel to the mix—a different sound, perhaps, or a brand-new custom—but also sustains a tradition that is even older than the nation itself: the revitalizing effects of immigration upon religion. During the 17th century, the first surge of immigration to the New World brought Protestantism to these shores, imprinting its beliefs, as well as its architecture, on the landscape of an emerging nation. Subsequent waves of immigrants, many of them evangelical Protestants, furthered their faith's hold on the population throughout the 18th century even as they challenged its tenets from within.

With the arrival in the 19th century of large numbers of Catholic immigrants, the United States could no longer lay claim to being a Protestant nation; a largely Christian nation, yes, but not one whose moral compass was set entirely by Protestantism. Catholics, after all, had their own ideas about religion, morality, and living a good life. In changing America, Catholic immigrants from Italy and Ireland, Germany and Poland also changed the nature of the Roman Catholic Church in this country. Religion, they insisted, had as much to do with honoring Old World, ancestral traditions as with honoring churchly ones, prompting the church to rethink the relationship between faith and community. Meanwhile, as Roman Catholic churchmen sought to reckon with the growing power of ethnicity, and Protestant leaders sought to reckon with the staying power of Catholicism, Jewish immigrants challenged both groups. Arriving in the New World in large numbers at the very end of the 19th century and in the opening years of the 20th, the Jews were just as inclined to hold on to their own Old World customs as were their Italian Catholic counterparts. More important, they were non-Christians. The first sizable immigrant population not to believe in Jesus Christ or to venerate the New Testament, they broke the mold, compelling Christian America to extend its promise of religious freedom to those outside the fold. Eventually, after many fits and starts, it did. In the aftermath of World War II, Judaism took its place alongside Catholicism and Protestantism as an authentically American religious phenomenon or, as Will Herberg, one religious commentator, then put it: America today is a "three-religion country" in which Protestantism, Catholicism, and Judaism each in its own way represents the "American way of life."

Buddhists, Hindus, Sikhs, Jains, and Muslims, however, did not figure in this scheme of things. Neither Jewish nor Christian nor even Western, for that matter, they were set apart by history and geography; besides, there seemed to be few of them in America at the time. The post-1965 "new immigration" changed all that, however, rendering belief in a "three-religion country" out of date and out of touch with a contemporary America where religious diversity, not uniformity, had become the norm.

Through it all, amid a steady and unwavering succession of new faces, new ideas, and new faiths that have marked the American experience from the 17th century through the 20th, religion has been at the center of things. A link between the Old World and the New, between age-old traditions and new-found ones, religion has also challenged Americans to live up to the high ideals on which the nation was founded. If religious freedom flourishes today in America, and there is every reason to think that it does, we have the Bradfords and the Freys, the Kellys and the Cohens, the Hongs and the Itos, the Rodriguezes and the Kassams—immigrants all—to thank for it.

Chronology

1607

British settlers establish colony at Jamestown, Virginia, the first permanent settlement in the New World

1620

Pilgrims establish Plymouth Plantation

1630

Puritans leave England for the Massachusetts Bay Colony

1630s–1640s

Era of the Puritan Migration

The colony of Maryland is established

1636

Religious reformer Anne Hutchinson is tried and convicted for her beliefs; she is banished from the Massachusetts Bay Colony

1649

Maryland passes "An Act Concerning Religion," granting all Christians equality under the law

1681

William Penn establishes Pennsylvania as a "holy experiment"

Huguenots settle in South Carolina

1683

Mennonites settle in Germantown, Pennsylvania

1730s

Amish and Moravians emigrate to Pennsylvania

The Seventh Day German Baptist Brethren establish Ephrata, Pennsylvania

1750s

Moravians settle in Salem, North Carolina

1782

French diplomat J. Hector St. John de Crèvecoeur publishes *Letters from an American Farmer,* extolling freedom in America

1820s

Norwegians begin to settle in the Midwest

1840s

Era of large-scale German and Irish immigration to America

1850s

Chinese immigrants settle in California during the Gold Rush; establish first Chinatown in San Francisco

1854
Rabbi Isaac Mayer Wise brings Reform Judaism to Cincinnati

1870s
Era of German Catholic and Swedish Protestant immigration

1879
Dedication of St. Patrick's Cathedral in New York City draw worshipers from across the country

1880s
Mass immigration of Italians and eastern European Jews to United States begins

Japanese settle in the West

1882
U.S. passes the Chinese Exclusion Act, halting Chinese immigration for 10 years

The festival honoring the Madonna of Mount Carmel is inaugurated in New York City, introducing religious street processions to the United States

1887
Eldridge Street Synagogue on New York's Lower East Side is dedicated, reportedly the first synagogue built by eastern European immigrants

1893
World's Parliament of Religions is held in Chicago; a showcase of unity among differing religious beliefs

1898
Young Men's Buddhist Association is formed in San Francisco

1900–1920
Immigrants from Korea and Mexico settle in the United States

1905
Jews celebrate the 250th anniversary of Jewish settlement in America in Carnegie Hall, New York City

1921–1924
United States severely restricts immigration from Europe and Asia by establishing quotas

1930s

German Jews seek asylum in the United States

1940s

U.S. government places Japanese Americans in internment camps throughout the United States following the Japanese attack on Pearl Harbor on December 7, 1941

1946–1964

Era of the Great Migration of Puerto Ricans

1948

U.S. passes the Displaced Persons Act, permitting World War II refugees to enter the country

1960s

Cubans emigrate in large numbers to the United States, especially to Florida

1965

U.S. relaxes curbs on immigration, allowing people from Southeast Asia, the Far East, and the Middle East to enter

1970s

Haitians seek refuge in the United States

Immigration of Soviet Jews begins

1973

Shrine to Our Lady of Charity is consecrated in Miami, a focal point for Cuban refugees throughout the nation

1981

Sree Venkateshwara Temple (Hindu shrine) opens its doors in Malibu, California

1990s

Jews from the former Soviet Union continue to emigrate

Muslims in America establish more than 1,000 mosques and Islamic centers

1993

U.S. Supreme Court rules in favor of animal sacrifices by the practitioners of Santeria in the case *The Church of Lukumi* v. *Hialeah*

Further Reading

GENERAL

Ahlstrom, Sidney. *A Religious History of the American People.* New Haven: Yale University Press, 1972.

Butler, Jon, and Harry S. Stout, eds. *Religion in American History: A Reader.* New York: Oxford University Press, 1997.

Gaustad, Edwin S. *A Religious History of America.* Rev. ed. San Francisco: Harper & Row, 1990.

Marty, Martin. *Pilgrims in Their Own Land: 500 Years of Religion in America.* New York: Penguin, 1985.

THE PROTESTANT IMMIGRANT EXPERIENCE

Alderfelder, E. G. *The Ephrata Commune: An Early American Counterculture.* Pittsburgh: University of Pittsburgh Press, 1985.

Blegen, Theodore C. *Norwegian Migration to America, 1825–1861.* 2nd ed. Northfield, Minn.: Norwegian-American Historical Association, 1969.

———— ed. *Land of Their Choice: The Immigrants Write Home.* Minneapolis: University of Minnesota Press, 1955.

Butler, Jon. *Awash in a Sea of Faith: Christianizing the American People.* Cambridge: Harvard University Press, 1990.

Conzen, Kathleen Neils. *Immigrant Milwaukee.* Cambridge: Harvard University Press, 1976.

Crèvecoeur, J. Hector St. John de. *Letters from an American Farmer.* New York: Oxford University Press, 1997.

Earle, Alice Morse. *The Sabbath in Puritan New England.* 1891. Reprint, Detroit: Omnigraphics, 1998.

Fogelman, Aaron Spencer. *Hopeful Journeys: German Immigration, Settlement, and Political Culture in Colonial America, 1717–1775.* Philadelphia: University of Pennsylvania Press, 1996.

Gollin, Gillian Lindt. *Moravians in Two Worlds: A Study of Changing Communities.* New York: Columbia University Press, 1967.

Hall, David. *Worlds of Wonder, Days of Judgement: Popular Religious Belief in Early New England.* New York: Knopf, 1989.

MacMaster, Richard. *Land, Piety, Peoplehood: The Establishment of Mennonite Communities in America, 1683–1790.* Scottsdale, Penn.: Herald Press, 1985.

Morgan, Edmund S. *The Puritan Dilemma: The Story of John Winthrop.* Boston: Little, Brown, 1958.

————. *The Puritan Family: Religion and Domestic Relations in Seventeenth-Century New England.* New York: Harper, 1966.

Norton, Mary Beth. *Founding Mothers and Fathers: Gendered Power and the Forming of American Society.* New York: Vintage, 1996.

Remnick, David. "Bad Seeds." *New Yorker,* July 20, 1998, pp. 28–33.

Schneider, Carl E. *The German Church on the American Frontier.* St. Louis: Eden, 1939.

Sensbach, Jon F. *A Separate Canaan: The Making of an Afro-Moravian World in North Carolina, 1767–1840.* Chapel Hill: University of North Carolina Press, 1998.

Stephenson, George. *The Religious Aspects of Swedish Immigration: A Study of the Immigrant Churches.* 2nd ed. Minneapolis: University of Minnesota Press, 1972.

Thorp, Daniel B. *The Moravian Community in Colonial North America: Pluralism on the Southern Frontier.* Knoxville: University of Tennessee Press, 1989.

THE CATHOLIC IMMIGRANT EXPERIENCE

Brandenburg, Broughton. *Imported Americans: The Story of the Experiences of a Disguised American and His Wife Studying the Immigration Question.* New York: Frederick A. Stokes, 1904.

Chenault, Lawrence. *The Puerto Rican Migrant in New York City.* New York: Columbia University Press, 1938.

Diner, Hasia. *Erin's Daughters in America: Irish Immigrant Women in the 19th Century.* Baltimore: Johns Hopkins University Press, 1983.

Dolan, Jay P. *The Immigrant Church: New York's Irish and German Catholics, 1815–1865.* Baltimore: Johns Hopkins University Press, 1975.

————. *The American Catholic Experience: A History from Colonial Times to the Present.* Garden City, N.Y.: Doubleday, 1985.

Handlin, Oscar. *Boston's Immigrants, 1790–1865: A Study in Acculturation.* Cambridge: Harvard University Press, 1941.

McCarthy, Mary. *Memories of a Catholic Girlhood.* New York: Harcourt, Brace & World, 1957.

McDannell, Colleen. *Material Christianity: Religion and Popular Culture in America.* New Haven: Yale University Press, 1995.

McLane, Daisann. "The Cuban-American Princess." *New York Times Magazine,* February 26, 1995, pp. 42–43.

McLeod, Christian [Anna C. Ruddy]. *The Heart of the Stranger: A Story of Little Italy.* New York: Fleming H. Revell, 1908.

Morris, Charles K. *American Catholic: The Saints and Sinners Who Built America's Most Powerful Church.* New York: Times Books, 1997.

Orlean, Susan. "Old Fashioned Girls." *New Yorker,* February 12, 1990, pp. 82–88.

Orsi, Robert Anthony. *The Madonna of 115th Street: Faith and Community in Italian Harlem, 1880–1950.* New Haven: Yale University Press, 1985.

Riis, Jacob A. *How the Other Half Lives: Studies among the Tenements of New York.* Cambridge: Harvard University Press, 1970. 1st ed. 1890.

Rodriguez, Richard. *Hunger of Memory: The Education of Richard Rodriguez—An Autobiography.* Boston: Godine, 1982.

Sanchez, George. *Becoming Mexican-American: Ethnicity, Class and Identity in Chicano Los Angeles, 1900–1945.* New York: Oxford University Press, 1993.

Shaughnessy, Gerald. *Has the Immigrant Kept the Faith?* New York: Macmillan, 1925.

Stevens, Maria Diaz. *Oxcart Catholicism on Fifth Avenue: The Impact of the Puerto Rican Migration upon the Archdiocese of New York.* Notre Dame, Ind.: University of Notre Dame Press, 1993.

Sumrall, Amber Coverdale, and Patrice Vecchione, eds. *Catholic Girls.* New York: Penguin, 1992.

Tweed, Thomas A. *Our Lady of the Exile: Diasporic Religion at a Cuban Catholic Shrine in Miami.* New York: Oxford University Press, 1997.

VODOU (VOODOO) AND SANTERIA

Brown, Karen McCarthy. *Mama Lola: A Vodou Priestess in Brooklyn.* Berkeley: University of California Press, 1991.

———. "Judge: City Can Ban Sacrifice." *Miami Herald,* October 6, 1989, p. 1 [B].

———. "Sharing a Saint." *New York Times,* July 23, 1995, p. 13 [5].

———. "Court, Citing Religious Freedom, Voids a Ban on Animal Sacrifice." *New York Times,* June 12, 1993, p. 1.

———. "Santeria Faithful Hail Court Ruling." *New York Times,* June 13, 1993, p. 34.

THE JEWISH IMMIGRANT EXPERIENCE

Bernheimer, Charles Seligman. *The Russian Jew in the United States: Studies of Social Conditions in New York, Philadelphia and Chicago with a Description of Rural Settlements.* Philadelphia: J. C. Winston, 1905.

Cahan, Abraham. "The Late Rabbi Joseph, Hebrew Patriarch of New York." *American Monthly Review of Reviews* (September 1902): 311–14.

Gay, Peter. *My German Question: Growing Up in Nazi Germany.* New Haven: Yale University Press, 1998.

Gay, Ruth. *Unfinished People: Eastern European Jews Encounter America.* New York: Norton, 1996.

Helmreich, William B. *Against All Odds: Holocaust Survivors and the Successful Lives They Made in America.* New York: Simon & Schuster, 1992.

Howe, Irving. *World of Our Fathers: The Journey of the East European Jews to America and the Life They Found and Made.* New York: Harcourt Brace Jovanovich, 1976.

———. "Jewish Celebration Full of Enthusiasm," *New York Times,* December 1, 1905, p. 1.

Joselit, Jenna Weissman. *The Wonders of America: Reinventing Jewish Culture, 1880–1950.* New York: Hill & Wang, 1995.

Kertzer, Morris. "What Is a Jew?" *Look,* June 17, 1952, p. 120–28.

Kirchheimer, Gloria DeVidas, and Manfred Kirchheimer. *We Were So Beloved: The Autobiography of a German Jewish Community.* Pittsburgh: University of Pittsburgh Press, 1997.

Lowenstein, Steven M. *Frankfurt on the Hudson: The German-Jewish Community of Washington Heights, 1933–1983, Its Structure and Culture.* Detroit: Wayne State University Press, 1989.

Markowitz, Fran. *A Community in Spite of Itself: Soviet Jewish Emigres in New York.* Washington, D.C.: Smithsonian Institution Press, 1993.

Sarna, Jonathan, ed. *People Walk on Their Heads: Moses Weinberger's "Jews and Judaism in New York."* New York: Holmes & Meier, 1982.

Wise, Isaac Mayer. *Reminiscences.* Ed. and trans. David Philipson. New York: Central Synagogue of New York, 1945.

IMMIGRANTS OF THE LATE 20TH CENTURY

Bacon, Jean. *Life Lines: Community, Family and Assimilation among Asian Indian Immigrants.* New York: Oxford University Press, 1996.

Garcia, Kenneth J. "Sight to Behold: Ornate Hindu Temple in Malibu Is Shrine Where East Meets West." *Los Angeles Times*, March 25, 1988, p. 2 [1].

Goodstein, Laurie. "At Camps, Young U.S. Sikhs Cling to Heritage." *New York Times,* June 18, 1998, p. A1.

Haddad, Yvonne Yazbeck, and Adair T. Lummis. *Islamic Values in the United States: A Comparative Perspective.* New York: Oxford University Press, 1987.

Kingston, Maxine Hong. *The Woman Warrior: Memoirs of a Girlhood among Ghosts.* New York: Knopf, 1975.

Ostling, Richard. "One Nation Under God: Not Without Conflict, An Unprecedented Variety of Faiths Blooms Across the Land." *Time,* Fall 1993, pp. 62–63.

Smith, Jane I. *Islam in America.* New York: Columbia University Press, 1999.

Takaki, Ronald. *Strangers from a Different Shore: A History of Asian Americans.* Rev. ed. Boston: Back Bay Books, 1998.

———. "To Asian Refugees, United States Is Still the Land of Hope." *New York Times,* June 28, 1986, p. 1.

Williams, Raymond B. *Religions of Immigrants from India and Pakistan: New Threads in the American Tapestry.* New York: Cambridge University Press, 1988.

Index

Acknowledgments

A collaborative effort in the very best sense of the word, the writing of this book benefited from several pairs of hands and eyes. For their sensitivity to both history and language, I would like to thank Kaari Ward, my project editor, and Katherine Adzima, managing editor at Oxford University Press. Nancy Toff, editorial director at Oxford, enlivened matters with her keen sense of humor and equally keen critical imagination, as did the searching questions of series editor Jon Butler. I am most grateful to Professor Butler for giving me the opportunity to read widely and to think long and hard about the soul of this country.

Picture Credits

Aga Khan Visual Archives, MIT. Ahmed Nabal, 1999: 117; International News Photos, courtesy AIP Emilio Segre Visual Archives: 92; AP/ WIDE WORLD PHOTOS: 42; Courtesy of the Boston Public Library, Print Department: 2, 46, 70; Brown Brothers: 55; California Historical Society, FN-13890: 101; Carnegie Hall Archives: 80; Courtesy Catholic Archives of Texas, Austin: 44; Chantal Regnault: 68; Chicago Historical Society: 53, 75; Chicago Jewish Archives, Spertus Institute of Jewish Studies: 79; Cincinnati Medical Heritage Center: 78; Cincinnati Museum Center Image Archives: 83; Martha Cooper/ City Lore: 65, 66, 114; Congregation Beth Israel, Houston, Texas: 90; Culver Pictures: 25; Copyright the Dorothea Lange Collection, Oakland Museum of California, City of Oakland. Gift of Paul S. Taylor: 40; Craig Benner, Photographer, Ephrata Cloister, Pennsylvania Historical and Museum Commission: 35; Photo by Don Farber: 109; By Permission of the Folger Shakespeare Library: 24; Photographer Lewis W. Hine. Courtesy George Eastman House: 10; Hebrew Immigrant Aid Society: 94; Hindu Temple of Atlanta: 98; Art by A. Manivelu. Courtesy of Hinduism Today Magazine, Hawaii: 115; The Historic New Orleans Collection, accession no. 1979.277.1: 48; The Jacob Rader Marcus Center of the American Jewish Archives: 81; Library of Congress: 6 (POS-WWI-US no.251), 12-13 (USZ62-44048), 23, 29 (USZ62-53348), 30 (USF34- 82410-E), 31 (USZ62-99492), 33 (USZ62-31861), 47 (USZ62-31649/412490), 61 (USF34-009950-C), 63 (USF34-32450), 77 (USZ62-30768); Shades of L.A. Archives/ Los Angeles Public Library: 89, 96, 107, 110, 111, 112; Colleen McDannell: 57, 59; Minnesota Historical Society: 49; Montana Historical Society, Helena: 85; "Bay and Harbor of New York" (detail), by Samuel B. Waugh, Courtesy Museum of the City of New York: cover; Bequest of Maxim Karolik, 1964, Courtesy Museum of Fine Arts, Boston. Reproduced with permission. ©2000 Museum of Fine Arts, Boston. All Rights Reserved: 27; National Archives: 103 (306-NT-1649990); National Archives-Pacific Region: 106 (NRHS-85-ISSF-AARCAS-14676(9)5-3); The Sowers, Index of American Design, Photograph © 2000 Board of Trustees, National Gallery of Art, Washington, c.1939, oil on board: 39; New York Public Library Picture Collection: 16, 19, 28; New York Public Library Rare Book Collection, ASTOR, LENOX and TILDEN Foundations: 32; Onondaga Historical Association, Syracuse, NY: 22; Oregon Historical Society: 87 (OrHi 25946); Presbyterian Historical Society, Presbyterian Church (U.S.A.)(Philadelphia): 120; Photo by Annie Wells, © The Press Democrat, Santa Rosa, CA: 60; Photo by Yale Strom, from his book The Hasidim of Brooklyn: A Photo Essay, Published by Jason Aronson: 95; Courtesy of Temple B'nai Israel, Rabbi Jimmy Kessler, Galveston, Texas: 73; Wells Fargo Bank: 102; Yale University: 20 (The Harold Wickliffe Rose Collection); The York County Heritage Trust, PA: 37.

Text Credits

The sidebars in the Religion in American Life series contain extracts of historical documents. Source information on sidebars in this volume is as follows:

"The Mission of the Puritans," p. 21: John Winthrop, "A Modell of Christian Charity" (1630), Michael Warner, ed., *American Sermons: The Pilgrims to Martin Luther King, Jr.* (New York: Library of America, 1999).

"Going to Parochial School," p. 50: Mary McCarthy, *Memories of a Catholic Girlhood* (New York: Harcourt, Brace, 1957).

"The December Dilemma," p. 88: Emil G. Hirsch, "How A Jew Regards Christmas," *Ladies' Home Journal,* December 1906, p. 10.

"Transmitting Tradition," p. 104: Maxine Hong Kingston, *The Woman Warrior: Memoirs of a Girlhood among Ghosts* (New York: Knopf, 1976). © 1975 and 1976 Maxine Hong Kingston. Reprinted by permission of Alfred A. Knopf, a division of Random House, Inc.

Jenna Weissman Joselit

Jenna Weissman Joselit is a visiting professor at Princeton University. She is the author of *The Wonders of America: Reinventing Jewish Culture, 1880–1950*, which received the National Jewish Book Award in History. Her latest book, *A Perfect Fit: Clothes, Character, and The Promise of America* will be published in 2001.

Jon Butler

Jon Butler is the William Robertson Coe Professor of American Studies and History and Professor of Religious Studies at Yale University. He received his B.A. and Ph.D. in history from the University of Minnesota. He is the co-author, with Harry S. Stout, of *Religion in American History: A Reader*, and the author of several other books in American religious history including *Awash in a Sea of Faith: Christianizing the American People*, which won the Beveridge Award for the best book in American history in 1990 from the American Historical Association.

Harry S. Stout

Harry S. Stout is the Jonathan Edwards Professor of American Christianity at Yale University. He is the general editor of the Religion in America series for Oxford University Press and co-editor of *Readings in American Religious History, New Directions in American Religious History, A Jonathan Edwards Reader*, and *The Dictionary of Christianity in America*. His book *The Divine Dramatist: George Whitefield and the Rise of Modern Evangelicalism* was nominated for a Pulitzer Prize in 1991.